I0840121

Don't dream it.

Be it.

Alexander Black

How to be Chinese

A step by step guide
how to survive and
enjoy the madness in China

Bibliografische Information der Deutschen
Nationalbibliothek:
Die Deutsche Nationalbibliothek verzeichnet diese
Publikation in der Deutschen Nationalbibliografie;
detaillierte bibliografische Daten sind im Internet über
www.dnb.de abrufbar.
© 2015 Alexander Black

Herstellung und Verlag:
BoD – Books on Demand, Norderstedt
ISBN: 978-3-7347-7079-1

Contents

An Introduction

Ah, dear Laowai 1, are you ready for becoming a true Chinese? You have an awesome journey ahead. China is amazingly big and the experiences you will have are mind-blowing. If somebody says he knows China, one of the first questions should be: What China? Northern China? Southern China? Chinese cities or the rural areas? Which minority? From my impression, there is no way that you ever can claim that you really understand this country as a whole.

I have described a lot of real-life situations in this book that you will probably experience pretty quickly after your arrival, no matter which area you're living in– and even years after staying here, you will still run into them and they will bring a smile on your face. Or make you bang your head against the wall due to frustration. But staying here for some while is totally worth it. From my experience, there are three types of foreigners who come here: The ones who hate this country, which is a very small share. The ones who are somehow ambivalent, this is also a very small share. And the ones who start to love it after their arrival. The ones who say "I just want to stay for a few months or years" but somehow get hooked up and will either not leave or always come back. It is a little bit like trying alcohol the first time: Maybe in the beginning

---

1   „Old Outsider" – you will probably hear this a lot on the streets, at least as long as you are outside the major tourist spots

you do not like the taste. But you will drink again and again. And maybe end up an alcoholic.

After staying here for a long time there is something I refer to as the "Asian trance". When something is happening around you even after years of being here you will have the feeling that you are totally lost in the events and just cannot grasp the situation evolving around you – but you will love it. You will have tears of joy in your eyes and will be so happy that you have had the opportunity to experience this. This is the moment when the trance sets in. There are also lots of dark sides where you have no idea what is happening, but this time you will hate it to an extent that you want to leave the country as quickly as possible while cursing at everybody crossing your way. Situations that will make you think that all of this intercultural experience is too much for you to bear and you want to smash everything around you. Luckily, these kinds of situations are much less frequent than the mind-boggling happy ones.

The most important recommendation I can give you is this: Be patient. Observe, relax, and if something does not work out the way you want it to work out there will be a solution, even if it might take some time. Calming down mostly helps.

One of the reasons to come here is that this country is a ride on a rocket – development compared to other countries is on light-speed which can be seen in construction, politics, but also culture. Some of the information I read in some traveler guides or culture bucks seems to be outdated, at least for the bigger cities. This country consists of long-lived traditions which are confronted with modern influence – you can clearly see that China was literally shot from stone-age to modern age in just a few decades. Sometimes people seem to be lost here on the way but somehow they all cope with the quick change. A change that at least for people who come from more tranquil places might be too much to bear with. But do not give up hope, dear Laowai with a big nose. You also somehow can enter the flow and get used to this firework of everyday-changes and development. And I promise, if you'll stay here long enough you'll find your old life in your old country boring.

And last but not least, in my opinion no foreigner can take this country really serious. Most foreigners who come here switch on their party mode, what happens in China stays in China anyway, and when they finally leave the country they switch it off again. This is an amusement park for adults where you can gaze in amazement at a great show somebody delivers on the street, and where you can shout out of horror because something is not going the way you've planned it. But still, it is an amusement park with lots and lots of different experiences waiting for you to discover.

I love it. At some point I might hate it. But until then I will enjoy every day here and be happy that I have the chance to spend a share of my life in this amazing country. And I hope you will too.

An Ordinary Business Trip

This book could probably consist solely of a short story about a very ordinary business trip I've had. Almost everything I want to share with you is included in that story already. Yet you would rightly be enraged about the fact that you had invested in a book with only three pages. So let's hold a challenge instead – I challenge you to read my description of the business trip which I tried to keep as neutral as possible. Afterwards, read the rest of the book. And in the end come back and try to find as many of the things that you've learned about. It will be easy if you know what you have to look for. Here we go:

I've just received information that I will be going on a spontaneous business trip to a city far away from every airport in the middle of China. I have nothing except an airplane ticket and a vague idea that I might be back a few days later.

One of my colleagues grabs me in the office and we drive to the airport where he steers me in a very routinely manner, including jumping the queue, through the check-in procedures with a short break at the business lounge until we get on the plane. Arriving at the destination airport we get picked up by a driver and off it goes. About 2 hours later our driver gets a call informing him that the key to another car the company that invited us for the journey needs is in our car. No problem, since we just saw a bus on its way to the very city the key should go to and - after very short negotiations - the bus driver agrees to take the car key with him.

While we are sitting in the car, we pass other cars from which somebody is throwing plastic bottles out of the window. Finally we arrive at our location and get checked in our simple hotel – obviously I will be sharing a room with my Chinese colleague for the business trip. Since I've mentioned that I have a dry throat from air conditioning he recommends drinking a lot of hot water to make it better again.

Shortly after our arrival, we get picked up again by the driver and we are driven to the local government where our client and some important government officials are waiting for us. While drinking tea, heavy smoking in the room, and hearing how good my Chinese is several times we finally start dinner – as the most important person here today I get the chair facing the door and the honor to drink a lot of the local liquor called Baijiu and some red wine. Surrounding me I can hear a concert of people enjoying their food without closing their mouths and slurping in the noodles. One of the guys in there is not only proud of his drinking skills, but also proud that he can smoke 3 packs of cigarettes a day.

My boss is also mentioned with appraisal, especially since he is also really good at drinking. Some people who are not considered to be important managers are serving us all the time: Filling up the glasses, bringing in a lot of food, and basically doing everything the important guys tell them to do.

After a few hours of eating, drinking and chatting we can finally return to the hotel – we had just finished brushing our teeth, taking a shower, and my colleague finished taking a pretty noisy dump in the bathroom when there's a knock on the door: Some other important government officials did not show up so we can change our room from "normal type" to "executive type". While trying to fall asleep on the still very hard but a bit more comfortable bed I can hear people out in the hallway walking and talking, and someone is playing music all night which spatial origin I cannot even locate. Either way, I roll up some tissues and put them in my ears to finally fall asleep.

Next morning at 6:30 we are picked up again for breakfast, which once again is served at the local government. This breakfast of course already involves a lot of smoking. We then set off back to the hotel again, where some busses are waiting for the around 600 people participating in this event – the opening of a new facility. On our bus drive to the location we see lots and lots of police and army presence making sure that our convoy can pass without a problem. Meanwhile some tour guide is entertaining us with some information regarding local history and singing local songs to us.

The first stop is a memorial for Chairman Mao – we visit this place for about half an hour and our tour guide not only takes care that we keep together but also proudly shows us the bed in which Mao slept for one night, a stone in which with a certain degree of imagination you can read his name, and we all bow in front of a Mao statue.

Off we go again to the facility where they have constructed a big stage for the opening ceremony to take place. There is also a smaller stage where some people can watch the show from the front and as a guest of honor I get my own place there while all the other people I know have to find a place somewhere else. After about 45 minutes of speeches the local middle school performs an impressive drum show on stage, followed by the elementary school with some kind of dance and some singers singing and dancing.

After the show we have about 30 minutes to visit the newly opened museum – in order to keep the regular people out the doors are locked with a chain behind us. And of course some of the guests are smoking in this museum.

After this visit is over we have some time left to have a look at the surrounding park where first government officials and people from other companies, and then local private visitors seize the opportunity to take a picture of themselves with my foreign face.

Next stop is lunch where we get served some local special food which is highly appreciated by every participant and again have some time to take a walk – somewhere we find a rock which says that Mao sat on it. That is why it has now the form of a sofa.

On the way back to the museum we pass a small market where you can buy local vinegar and Baijiu. This time we go to the meeting room inside the museum: I was asked to prepare a presentation about our company without any information how long it should last – anything between 10 to 60 minutes. Obviously it gets cancelled since other people have prepared lengthy speeches anyway. Some people around me just take a nap while sitting. After the one-hour-meeting we go outside again, sit in the museum, and some of the people with me are smoking again.

Finally it is time for the closing ceremony – the police and army presence is pretty impressive. As a guest of honor I again get a nice seat in the second row directly behind the local government. Again, the ceremony begins with speeches. And at precisely that moment, at which a government official mentions the long and highly developed culture of China, a child squats down in front of me surrounded by hundreds of people and takes a shit.

The performance starts: It is basically the same as in the morning, but this time they added some more famous singers from all over China. While many people around are clapping and cheering and waving to the performers, the local government officials are sitting there without any facial expressions whatsoever. Finally, the climax of the show: A famous star sings songs and the police is unable to restrain the crowd anymore as they jump up and run to the stage, even in front of the local government officials who are still motionless.

The show is over; we return to our busses and drive back to the local government for dinner, drinking. And smoking. My colleague somehow manages to rescue me from drinking too much Baijiu by telling the people that in my culture beer is much more accepted: So I just swallow down glass after glass of beer since everybody wants to drink with me while next to me the chain smokers are once again enjoying their cigarettes. The level of noise gets really high again and everybody is shouting nice words to each other.

At around midnight we return to the hotel.

On the third day we get up at around eight for breakfast which again involves heavy smoking by some guys and drinking tea afterwards. Suddenly, very suddenly indeed, the atmosphere changed from "relationship building" to "business" – my colleague discussed business matters with the leader, while servants are jumping back and forth filling up glasses of tea and handing out cigarettes to everybody. About half an hour later the business is obviously concluded and we visit some other facility in which they want to use our products in the future. About ten people are standing around and discussing where exactly to put it.

Since business is concluded we excuse ourselves and return to the driver who brings us to another airport. Since we tried to make a reservation for plane tickets in the afternoon the driver uses some covers for the license plates in order for the speed cameras to not catch his license plates while speeding. Since the roads are under construction here nobody is really sure where to go – and even if there is a sign that the new highway is still under construction, we try to get on it until finally being stopped by some big rocks on the way and turning back.

We arrive at the airport just in time – unfortunately it turns out that we have tickets for a plane two hours later. My colleague invites me and the driver for lunch at a local street restaurant, where a 12-year-old boy stares at me and is somehow so surprised to see a Chinese-speaking foreigner that he freezes until we can make him move and talk again.

He is barely able to say more than 3 sentences in English – but still my Chinese colleague mentions how smart he is. I ask the boy for how long he's been studying English: Obviously for 5 years already.

We finally can get to the airport, enter the airplane, and fly back. As soon as the plane's rear tires touch the ground I see many people switching on their phones and opening their safety belts not really caring that we are still travelling at a speed of hundreds of kilometers per hour.

We get out of the airport where our driver is waiting for us already. While I somehow managed to evade this my Chinese colleague has yet another business dinner tonight.

Three days after leaving the city I live in I am back at home. And again I am flashed by things happening in this country.

You have no idea what happened in this story? And no idea what lessons you should learn from it? Well, let's get ready for the steps to become Chinese.

1 Become Selfish – You and Your Social Group Come First

First things first: You should forget everything you have ever learned about being polite or considerate in your childhood. This is a treat you will not really see here very often with people you do not know. Maybe the local amazing citizens will be a bit more considerate to you since you do not have a Chinese face, but otherwise you should not expect too much politeness over here. But since this guide is designed to be a very practical one I guess it is the best to show you real-life-situations of how it is done.

Is there a better way to find out how selfish somebody is than having a look at a situation with many people wanting something – and to find out who is waiting to get it and who is not? You think standing in a line while waiting your turn is fun?

Well, here in China there are no queues – even if you think there is one it is more a ball of chaotic madness where people always try to be the first. When in Rome do as the Romans do: Extend your elbows and push everybody is threatening your position in line back. Jumping the queue is sports here. You can start to imagine that the queue is more a big crowd where everybody pushes. It gets especially interesting while entering and exiting the subway: Nobody lets the people from the inside get out first, everybody pushes inside the carriage while the people from the inside are trying to push themselves out. So put your "pushing"-face on, pretend you do not see the pain you might cause to others, and push as hard as you can. This game can also be played at a much smaller scale in an elevator: Push in, push out. And most importantly do not forget to push the "close the door"-button even if you see somebody running to catch the elevator. He might take away the personal space that you really need while he has "just" to wait for 5 minutes again. And since you should not put too much trust in the buttons anyway be sure to press the button as many times as possible until the door is really closed. Letting other people not get into the elevator is especially fun in one of the 30-stories high living buildings with only 3 elevators.

And not only in an actual queue is it an interesting experience to push others: Did you ever wonder why traffic is so chaotic here? If you look around some drivers just park their cars in the middle of the street while other drivers block each other because nobody wants to give way to anybody else. Basically there is one rule about driving a car here: The one who is least scared about getting a scratch in his car wins. Thus, a crucial recommendation if you do not always want to lose the battle on the street: Get a rental car. If it's a rental, don't be gentle. Of course if an accident actually happens you will have a lot of bystanders – but nobody will help. It does not matter if somebody is brutally beaten up in a restaurant, if somebody gets hit in the traffic lying on the street without anybody calling emergency services. There will be lots of people standing around and watching with big interest but nobody will move a finger to help. Why is that? Well, some people say that this is the result of a weird court ruling: a person who was not involved in an accident and wanted to help was sentenced to pay compensation. There is absolutely no reason to help if you are guilt free. Other opinions include that there is never enough for everybody anyway, so by this "first come first serve, and do not care about anybody else"-rule this is again a self-organizing chaos with poor victims left behind.

Even a phenomenon that might seem cute for uninitiated foreigners can become a battle of selfishness. Did you ever hear about the dancing grannies? If not just go visit public places. If you checked enough places you will surely come across some grandmothers dancing to music originating from portable speakers. Cute you say? That is as long as you're not living next to them. Since these grannies also congregate next to residences their music and dancing can be a public nuisance. What begins with a one-hour-dancing session can quickly become a 12-hours-disco next to your living room, which can also massively influence the market value of the residence you've bought. Since these grannies are not really the kindest type any protest by people living next to their public music club is kindly or not so kindly discarded – and quickly this peaceful activity evolves into a war between residents and old people. The residents become creative in their way of fighting back, methods known hitherto include throwing feces at the dancers or investing an awful lot of money in special speakers intended for crowd control at demonstrations to shout back.

Anyway – just remember the rule: Be selfish, you come first.

Even though people here are selfish there is one other thing they are: They are group-oriented. Thus, selfishness can quickly develop into "groupishness" – but this is only true if you really know the other people well or you have a deep connection with them. Or want to have a deep connection with them. Or you have a lot of respect for them. Or there is some other reason.

Anyway, while selfishness is mostly the biggest driving factor here people can still suddenly become very protective and caring if you somehow belong to their social group. Which also means: If you do not belong to their social group you might get serious problems. Sometimes not only single people try to cut the line in front of you but a whole bunch of people pushes their way through. And I would certainly not recommend getting into a fight with locals here as a foreigner: Even bystanders who have nothing to do with a fight might join in – and as a non-Chinese person you should certainly not expect them to support you. You are more likely to feel a bottle break on your head. Crucial recommendation: Be peaceful. And while you can complain a lot here you should pretty much know where the limit is and stop there before somebody becomes a furious beast.

2 Love Chinese Food

If you have never been to the kingdom of the middle then you probably misunderstand the crap sold in Chinese restaurants in your country as "Chinese food". You are totally mistaken. Ignore the superstitions that all Chinese people are eating dog meat - dog meat is considered a specialty merely in some regions of China so there is lots of other food to choose from. While the people in southern China (around Guangdong) will probably eat everything with four legs except a table and everything with wings except an airplane, people from other regions sometimes do not really enjoy that kind of food. Either way, if you are looking for fried bees, scorpions, snakes, or any other weird things, you will find them if you look hard enough. But beware: this can be a hard task for you.

Since the country is having a hard time with lots of food scandals you will even eat things that you did not want to eat — and which are not really the healthiest. Some of the more recent scandals include mixing milk powder with unhealthy substances, selling rat meat instead of mutton, tweaking pig meat with chemicals for so long that it looked like beef, or my personal favorite, the so called "gutter oil". Some really smart people had the great idea that fat swims above water, so they went to the closest sewers and went fishing for some fat swimming there above the feces. After cooking it for a little while it was sold again as cheap oil, especially for the small street shops.

Let us stop looking at the partly true superstitions and focus more on the good Chinese food: Rice and Noodles are the basics here. You would think. Actually, while these components can be part of a simple meal in middle-class restaurants and upwards they are merely served in the end to fill the reminding free space you might have in your tummy. Even while the Chinese government is appealing to the people to reduce waste of food there is still a tendency of ordering too much food to be polite or even impress the people who are around you.

So much for the description of food. But since you are reading a guide on how to become Chinese you should consider these hints:

Learn how to eat with chopsticks. D'uh. This is too obvious I guess, but while some things seem to wrap themselves around the chopsticks and become really easy to eat other types of food might be really challenging, especially slim noodles in a soup. If you are not in one of the most plain restaurants ever the food will be in the middle of the table and everybody will pick what he or she wants with their own chopsticks. Try everything. If there are still bones mixed with the meat do not be afraid. This is common in many dishes. Ignore or appreciate the mode of presentation, e.g. the baked rabbit head smiling at you next to the remains of his baked body. Be happy that you get fresh food and don't forget that - especially in upper class restaurants - this poor animal in front of you may have been jumping or swimming around in front of your nose merely half an hour ago. Simply do not ask what you are eating. If somebody tells you that this food is "good for men" eat more of it to increase your sexual potency. Mostly it is simply some kind of vegetable, meat, or fruit that somehow resembles a stick.

When you come back from a trip and friends of you ask you how the trip went tell them that the food was really good. With this most Chinese people will be satisfied as an outline of your trip. And while eating, tell the others how good it tastes - and ask others, how good the food is. You can even let the people who are not with you right now enjoy what you are eating – looking at the pictures in social media according to my impression at least twenty percent of the postings are pictures of food somebody is eating somewhere.

Get used to eating spicy food. It is amazing and your mouth will get adapted to it. Maybe not your tummy, and you might spend a long time in the bathroom the next day. But your mouth will.

Do not bother to make no sounds while eating. If you are eating noodles in a soup and your mouth is pumping out a vacuum cleaner like sucking noise you have become truly local. And of course while chewing there is no need to close your mouth - let others enjoy the view of the food being squashed between your teeth.

Never ever let anything collide with your eating plans: Breakfast, Lunch and Dinner are the most important appointments on your entire day. If you have to skip one it is totally acceptable to be close to a panic attack. If it is two feel like Armageddon is coming fast.

3   Consume Alcohol and Cigarettes

Since we have thus far only covered the amazing Chinese food there is one other thing that usually goes hand in hand: Alcohol and cigarettes. Both are considered to be bad for women but as a true guy you have to show off your drinking skills. Especially as a foreigner you are expected to be a great drinker. There is no better way of showing off how masculine you are than demonstrating your skill in putting lots and lots of Baijiu in you. Baijiu is like the Chinese Vodka, it just tastes much worse.

If there is no Baijiu available that is not a problem - you can do "bottoms up" with every kind of drink: Beer, Wine, Red wine mixed with sprite, or Whiskey mixed with ice tea. There is no limit to creativity as long as there is alcohol included. If you want to show off how rich you are try to estimate how many of the most expensive drinks your group could drink within three days. Then order double the amount. If you have no space left on your table because it is full of bottles you did the right thing.

In a restaurant it is easy to recognize if people were having a good time: If the toilets are still completely clean at the end of an evening (or at the end of lunch time) and there is no vomit at all it must have been a boring restaurant or party.

The time of the day is also not an issue: If you are on your way to a business lunch, especially with officials or high ranking people, expect that you will come back drunk afterwards.

Drinking alcohol is a ritual which is not only considered as a fun activity but also as the primary mode of celebrating or bonding with people. Just a small warning: You should know your limits. And by limits I am not talking about the point of suffering from minor alcohol poisoning leading to vomiting since this can be seen as an indicator for having fun. I'm talking about the major alcohol poisoning that a government official suffered from after he got his new job and drank himself to death at the celebration party. But almost every good party I have been to lately included somebody throwing up with somebody else patting their back in order to comfort them.

Very important: Bring your own cigarettes. And smoke. But to make it socially acceptable offer somebody else a cigarette first. And since you do not want to look cheap to them you shouldn't buy the cheapest cigarettes available: For a middle-class smoker it is acceptable to have cigarettes which cost around 3 times as much as the cheapest ones while as a government official it should be at least 10-15 times as expensive as the cheapest ones.

If somebody offers you a cigarette you should help them to light up theirs - and as soon as you finished smoking the free cigarette please do not forget to return the favor of offering one of yours to the other person. You can imagine how easy you will change from being an occasional smoker to a chain smoker during a meal.

Smoking is acceptable almost everywhere — save for special locations such as airports, subways, and big shopping malls. But in a restaurant, on the elevator, in a small store, or inside the taxi you can (mostly) light up directly next to the non-smoking sign. Only during the Olympic Games in 2008 and a few months afterwards the rule of non-smoking was enforced, yet after that everybody stopped caring again.

Since you cannot always eat something if you want to get hammered there are other great excuses you can use: Go to a bar, but be aware that bars are not considered "traditional" and you should never tell your parents that you went there. Going to Karaoke or KTV is totally acceptable on any time of the day. For everybody who has never seen a KTV: It is basically a bar with walls around each table (so that you cannot get in touch with somebody you don't know), a microphone, and a TV to select songs to sing. It is simply far more "traditional" and totally acceptable to go there.

If a lunch or dinner takes around 2 hours be prepared to be drunk afterwards and having smoked so many cigarettes that your lungs are burning.

Good news for girls in the end as a surprise: Do not participate in this. This is a guy´s game. No smoking, no drinking. This is just not traditional and girls should be traditional. Period.

4   Reconsider Your Views on Cleanliness

Thinking about cleanliness and hygiene in a country that is known for its increasing pollution on a big scale everywhere is a challenge itself. You have probably read the newspaper reports about the dirty air and the bad water quality. Even while this will affect your everyday life here, for example by influencing your decision to go running outside when the air pollution level is "hazardous" or by drinking the tap water, this is not what I want to talk about here.

Our scale right now is much smaller: Bathrooms. Come again you ask? What does that have to do with me?

Since going to the bathroom is one of the most basic needs anybody can have as a future inhabitant of China you will visit them a lot.

What do bathrooms look like? Bathrooms are basically everywhere. There are extremely public ones, meaning: Find a hidden tree. Or if you are a child, peeing on the sidewalk is also totally okay and according to a survey totally accepted by Chinese society "under certain conditions" – most children are running around in special pants with an open crotch anyway, making it easier to do their big and small businesses wherever they are. But if you are a child you should not be reading this guide. However, even if you are already an adult find a hidden or not-so-hidden-spot and go for it.

A little less public option is the bathroom in restaurants or their public counterparts on the street, sometimes but not always easily to be found by the bad smell they emit to their surroundings. Obviously, as a new Chinese you should not care too much for privacy: Do not expect that every bathroom has walls to separate the holes to take a dump in. If it has walls, do not expect them to be higher than half a meter. If they are, do not expect that there are doors. If you have a secluded cell with a door, you can consider yourself really lucky and in a high-class-bathroom no matter how bad the smell is. But since these bathrooms are not really the cleanliest the Chinese developed an amazing system: Squat toilets and the rule that you should never ever touch anything in there. The big advantage of a squat toilet is that not even your ass has to touch an unclean surface. The big disadvantage is that we as foreigners are not used to squatting so we probably will have to touch many a thing trying not to lose our balance. You should really learn how to squat properly before going there or you might fall down into the excrements of other people.

Since privacy in the bathroom is not known to everybody here always enter the toilet with a big smile: Sometimes you just see somebody squatting over the hole on the ground with a cigarette in one hand, his mobile phone in the other hand and a big smile in your direction on his face while his backside is taking care of the business. Smile back and be polite.

After you finished your business you will probably find out that there is no toilet paper - you should really bring your own. And dispose of it into the trash can next to the toilet, otherwise it might get stuck somewhere in the pipes.

On your way out you might also find out that there might be a sink but soap in a bathroom can be considered as pure luxury. If you really do not want to be too Chinese maybe you should carry around germicide to disinfect your hands. And just hope that everybody you are sharing the peanuts with in the bar also brought some.

If you have trash do not worry about where to find a trash can. The entire world is one. You have an empty bottle in your hand? Dump it anywhere. You don't know where to put the cigarette stub? Drop it anywhere, doesn't matter if you are inside of a restaurant or outside on the street. There are plenty people who have nothing else to do than pick up your trash - this is what they do for their living. The general rule is: If you don't need it, drop it. If you drop something by accident but you still need it - think about whether you really still want to do have it even after it touched the top of a trash can (which is basically everywhere in this world as you should remember by now). E.g. you are having a hard time with your chopsticks and your food drops onto the table in the restaurant? The table is not clean. Leave the food there. You've dropped the chopsticks themselves on the table? Ask for new ones like a professional.

5   Dress Up – Chinese Style!

While the style to dress up is pretty unique for guys and girls, there is one thing that you can do no matter your gender: Throw away the razor. You will not need it. It does not really matter what kind of hair we are talking about, whether it's the hair under the arms, on your legs or your pubic hair. Just grow your own small rainforest there. To be fair, Chinese people mostly do not have not a strong growth of hair in most of these areas anyway but who cares. And not to forget the occasional really long hair growing out of a mole – which might be a pretty upsetting view for the uninitiated. And that girls sometimes have a more impressive mustache than guys is also something you should get used to while guys sometimes prefer to have long nostril hair.

For guys it is easy to dress up: Wear whatever you want. If it is really hot it should just be loose enough so you can run around topless or at least tie the shirt up on top of your belly button. And yes, do not ask – you can do that or even take off your shirt completely in a restaurant or any public place. No worries. A pajama is always helpful to do so. It is perfectly fine to use it in everyday situations.

The style at work might be a bit different – there are many jobs were you are required to wear a uniform, starting from police to other security guards, restaurants... whatever, there are so many jobs where you are required to wear a uniform that it might be easier to list the exceptions.

For girls the general rule is also pretty simple: Do it childish. Do it colorful. Do it sexy. No, there is no such thing as too much "Hello Kitty" or "SpongeBob" as long as the dress or the pants are short enough. Since Chinese girls are mostly small be sure to buy high heels – and there is no need for you to be able to walk in them. Most girls here cannot. And if you do not like high-heels you can buy shoes on plateaus in many shapes. It is almost surprising to see a girl not doing anything to make her look taller. And while you are at it add some incredibly cute bunny ears or at least some fake glasses without – well – glass inside. The other extreme to the childish sexy style is the great pajama look (again), which is incredibly popular for the people over 30 years old. If you go for a walk, shopping or on a date – with a pajama you can signal to everybody that you have an incredibly relaxed lifestyle.

Since part of the local population is getting richer and richer they want to separate themselves from the rural inhabitants in different kinds of ways. Incredibly popular are creams and lotions which will make you look pale – you will probably never see a tanning studio anywhere here. During summer you can also see a lot of people walking around with their umbrella to make sure that not too much sun touches their skin. White skin equals being beautiful. And if you happen to go to the seaside you might even come across people wearing "facekinis", an amazing mix between a mask for a bank robber and neoprene, which allows comfortable bathing including the feeling to get wet without the stupid side-effect of getting tanned at the same time.

Other options to set you apart from the people in the countryside include: Growing at least (one) finger nail really long. Yes, also as a guy. This way you can express that you do not have to do hard physical labor anymore.

If you are rich enough, you can also invest a little bit money into your body. There are different kinds of beauty treatments available which are useless, painful, expensive, or any combination of the above. Starting from "slimming massage" to the occasional operation of the eyelids to make the eyes bigger, giving somebody a "two-fold-eyelid" (which actually exists as a word in Chinese), or the operation to make the legs longer: Again, creativity is limitless.

6 Chinese Communication: Speak in a Chinese Way

This is the most obvious one. Learn Chinese. But what is Chinese? Chinese is a language that is not a language it all with a myriad of dialects you can be sure that even Chinese people from different parts of the country do not understand each other if they utilize their dialect. Universal everywhere in mainland China are the characters - with just a few thousands of them you will be able to read the newspaper. Easy, right? Did you ever wonder why there are always Chinese subtitles in Chinese movies? To make sure everybody understands the movie even if he does not understand the dialect. Since you are a newcomer to this amazing language nobody expects you to be able to speak too much of it. And even if you do, even if you talk to people in Chinese, they will answer in English or will not understand you, since your foreign face does not match the words escaping your food hole.

You will find that communication is a bit different here: Especially in written communication you cannot over-exaggerate the friendly words and feelings. Which by the way sometimes is totally different from the way people communicate in restaurants: Did you ever try to shout out "WAITRESS! BEER!" or "WAITRESS! RICE!" in your own country to get served? I guess most of the restaurants would kick you out the door at some point. Occasionally this is necessary in order to get served at some point during the evening. If you just sit at your table and say nothing you sometimes also just get nothing. And of course the waiters are not really the most silent ones either. In some restaurants they're shouting so loud at you when you enter that you might think you entered the wrong venue and they want you to get out as quickly as possible.

If at some point you feel the urge to complain there are two ways to do this: The first one is by shouting, because obviously shouting louder will make your opinion the right one. Another way is to use endless discussions in a very relaxed and calm voice to resolve things. You want an example? Here you go:

I bought a Chinese brand smartphone here in China in a big electronics market and tried to check if it is a fake one with all the information I found on the Internet. The phone seemed legit. I asked the shopkeeper if it is a real one – he confirmed. After taking it home I discovered that it is not when I tried to install a software update. Next day I went back to that market with a Chinese female friend who wanted to help me to resolve the issue. For the first 30 minutes I was listening relaxed to their conversation. The next thirty minutes I was not that relaxed anymore and sometimes threw in Chinese sentences that I knew – still polite. After 60 minutes in total I started to get angry and forgot politeness which my parents had taught me when I was young. After a total of 90 minutes of listening to them my face already had a burning sensation; my hands were shaking because of anger. And yes, after two hours of that stupid negotiation process I was extremely close to punching my fist right into the face of the shop owner while shouting at him a wild mix of English and Chinese sentences. About two and a half hours later we were finally at the end of the negotiation process. Successfully. My friend did it. Oh, and by the way – that electronic mall obviously has an officer who is responsible for complaints about fake products. But my Chinese friend emphasized that it would be much less trouble and much faster to discuss this with the shop owner without the officer. Not sure if it is true but to be honest: If this was the easy way how hard must the other one be?

You should also consider to use the right medium for conversation: While in everyday life shouting at each other is totally acceptable, not only for complaining as I've mentioned above, for longer distances or as a service provider it might not be the smartest idea, so you really need two tools: Number one is the well-known smartphone, which is available all over the world. If you do not have a Smartphone with QQ or WeChat installed you are not really reachable and might disappear from the radar of your friends. If you are lucky you will sometimes get old-fashioned short messages, but these two apps are really quite common. Since phone numbers and mail addresses sometimes just change here, at least with these two apps you are fully prepared to never lose your friends anymore because they bought a new SIM card.

Number two might be not that essential in everyday life, but if you want to be a service provider you should really get a walkie-talkie. As soon as you enter a barbershop, massage shop, restaurant, or any other place you will find yourself in a perfectly organized process of people showing you the way and communicating with each other via walkie-talkies. And come on, didn't you always want a remote-controlled army of service providers that you can boss around over the air? Buy one piece of this amazing technology and enjoy!

Anyway, when you are here the first time do not expect anyone to understand what you want to tell them in English. Always print out the hotel address in Chinese beforehand and grab a business card at the reception before leaving the hotel again. Otherwise you either might not arrive at the hotel or get lost in the city without any idea how to get back to your luggage.

7 Chinese Communication: Adjust the Topics

Since I do not expect you to speak Mandarin from the beginning let us focus more on the English conversations you will have. Basically, they always follow the same structure in the beginning and widen to various but still limited topics later. The first question you will always encounter is: "Where are you from?" followed by a "How long have you been in China" pretty soon. If your Mandarin is good enough to answer these two questions in Chinese you will first get the information that "your Chinese is really good". And that you are "really beautiful/handsome", depending on your gender.

You should really learn how to highlight the obvious. If you meet somebody who is exceptionally tall please tell him since he probably only hears it three times a day and might have forgotten it since the last time he was told. If somebody is overweight you should also tell the person directly, since nobody would ever get offended by this. After lunch time when you meet somebody first ask them if he/she has eaten. If somebody comes back from somewhere ask if he/she is back. If it is hot outside mention it at least four times a day. Ditto if it's cold. I guess you get the gist.

Even if you get used to this way of conversation you might be surprised how often you do not get a clear answer – since there is no real "yes" or "no" in Chinese there are many other ways you can take. While the easiest way to answer a "yes or no"-question would be to repeat the verb while optionally adding the negative form (e.g. the "did you eat enough to be full?" – "eaten full" or "not eaten full"), this might be too easy. There are various ways to say "more or less", "almost" – basically the two extremes are between "I am hungry to death" and "eaten full to death" with most of the possible answers somewhere in-between.

There are some questions that we might not want to discuss with random strangers on the street in our own country - how much is your salary? How many days of vacation do you have per year? How much does your apartment cost? Are you married? Do you have children, sisters, or brothers? How big is your penis? Okay, I have to admit the last one is rare - but you can still encounter it often enough to mention it here. Anyway, be prepared to answer these and prepare yourself to ask the weirdest questions you can possibly imagine. Since irony is not understood here all of them will be answered in all seriousness, maybe just not really directly.

And while we are at it: Do not try to crack any jokes. Local humor and Chinese Humor are pretty different from each other.

If you are regularly in touch with the Chinese people via chat software you should learn how to make "copy and paste"-conversations – in the morning ask if they got up. In the evening tell them to rest early. Basically it is always the same piece of information that you can recycle hundreds of times with various people. Save yourself some trouble and copy and paste the messages to reduce your typing.

8 Forget the Concept of Privacy or Private Life

While you might have heard that the western world is more centered on the individual the Chinese world is more centered on relationships between people or social circles. This sounds pretty interesting in theory, but in reality it might hit you that privacy is not valued as much as as it is in other countries.

When you ask your friends who their friends are, of course some of the friendships developed while being at school, but you will much more find out that colleagues also can become quite close friends here pretty quickly. Jobs and private relationships are much more connected with these relationships very often being interwoven.

I've already talked about toilets, where doors are either optional or not closed by the person who uses them. But also in other places you might find less privacy than you might have expected. While as a foreigner you might have the luxury that you have a room for yourself at university or at least just a double room, it is not uncommon that 6-8 people share a room for several years while being at university. Even after university it is not uncommon to live together with other people for several years in one room, at least if you do not have the chance to live with your parents. Since people are so used to having other people around them they might be pretty scared if suddenly everybody was gone, even if it was for just a short time. After taking along a Chinese friend of mine to travel she realized she wants to travel more by herself, too. Her first big goal was to go to Tianjin for a whole weekend, which is about one hour by train from the city she is living in, Beijing. She enjoyed the day there by herself but in the end instead of going to a hotel like planned she took a train back since she was too scared to sleep in the hotel alone. She was 26 at that time.

Talking about hotels, some of them are not really designed for privacy, too. The walls are sometimes thin as paper, and even if you cannot hear what is happening behind the wall you can almost always hear everything through the door. Sometimes this is pretty fun – when you walk along the hallway and can hear exactly who is having a party, who is having fun in bed right now, or who's snoring loudly. And during business trips it is also not very uncommon that two colleagues share a hotel room together.

Oh, and if you are here just for a short period of time and somebody feels like he has to watch after you: You will have some people around that will not leave your side. They will be around all the time and might take away the fun of experiencing the country by yourself. Your Chinese workmates, friends, or whatever your relationship with them is will take care of all the big and small things, they will spend their weekend with you and show you around no matter whether you want this or not. Your babysitter will not leave you alone until you are really tired or until you make very clear that you really want to be alone for a while and discover this amazing country yourself.

If you want to be Chinese you should get rid of the feeling that you need privacy sometimes at least to some extent. Don't be embarrassed if somebody comes up when you take a shower after swimming in a public swimming pool and gives you a full body inspection. At least when you are not in the first or second tier cities you should also be prepared for a lot of people looking at you all the time – get prepared for a staring contest. During the time I was working at a university in a small city I already got used to the ritual at lunch time that the cleaning ladies stopped their work to watch me having my lunch for about half an hour. Staring back did not help at all. I just got used to having spectators while trying to manage using the chopsticks with slippery food. Try to accept that some people of the same gender touch you in an awkward way and don't let go. While you are in a Chinese nightclub you might have nice encounters with people who will put their hand on yours while you are talking to them and not let go. And if you are a girl other girls might just grab you and walk with you along the sidewalk this way. Do not be scared, this is their nice way to tell you that they enjoy your company. Enjoy listening to the sounds of people living behind your walls and do not mind making your own noises to enrich this concert. And for the final stage, get comfortable with somebody living with you in the same room even if you do not know that person.

And most importantly: Do not only get used to this. As soon as somebody visits you while you are here in China give them the great feeling of having a babysitter around all day by not leaving their side even for a second. They will either appreciate it – or shout at you to get lost at some point.

9 Do Not Obey Rules of Others but Make your Own!

Obviously the inhabitants of this amazing country do not think there might be any reason for any rules – and I do not want to talk about traffic on the streets again. No, this time another mode of transportation will lead you to being a true Chinese: The airplane. You sometimes complain about people opening their safety belt before the seatbelt-sign has been switched off? This is just for beginners. A true China expert will open the safety belt on the runway while the plane is still driving faster than a race car, jump up, and try to get the carry-on-luggage even before the plane took the first turn. Of course switching off mobile phones – the most precious way of communication here – is not very popular either. And it doesn't matter how often the safety video, pilot, and stewardesses tell people to shut their stupid phones and electronic devices, including the phones in airplane mode, off – which is totally sufficient in other countries by the way. These messages are just meant for all other people around you but never for yourself. So even when your neighbor is told to shut off the phone – wait until the stewardess tells you again directly. Lighters and matches are by the way totally prohibited on flights – in the check-in baggage and in the carry-on baggage. At least I am sure that the switch-off-the-mobile-phone-rule and the do-not-bring-lighters-rule are totally the result of the Chinese government not trusting their own people to not do something stupid. They surely must know that if somebody in in possession of this stuff they will use it to do something very stupid.

Even without any tools there were some articles about a guy who thought the air was too sticky on the runway – so they opened the emergency exit to get some fresh air on the way to the runway. Another great example is the guy who opened the emergency exit to disembark faster.

To make it short: As long as there are rules which are not enforced people will not follow them. This might be true for your country too. But here it is of course much more extreme.

After you already understood that people never listen to any rules anyway, unless they are enforced, it is time for you to make up really great rules and be creative about the enforcement: You want to make sure that the election of the next Chinese president goes well without anybody disturbing it by using papers to spread unwelcome messages? Sure, let all taxis in all of Beijing take away the handle of their windows, so that nobody can open the window while he is around. You want to make sure that people only get in and out of the taxi on the safe side, away from the road? Make it impossible to open the left door.

You want to pay the taxes for your apartment in the local taxation bureau? Without passport and some supplementing documents you are not allowed to give your money to this amazing country. Your loss, poor tax-payer, we do not want your money! You want to make sure that the university students are not tempted too much by nightlife? Lock the doors at 11:30 p.m. to make sure nobody gets in or out. You want to make sure that nobody uses a kitchen knife as the next weapon of mass destruction? Implement a rule that you can only buy a kitchen knife if you bring your passport. There have been some serious terrorist attacks by people using knives – but how the passport-checking-rule is going to prevent them is not really clear to me yet.

Sometimes it seems to be appreciated if somebody tells you what to do – you should really go to some kind of local activity to enjoy the Chinese way: For celebrations or shows there is always somebody there who will tell you that "the activity starts now" – and of course they also tell you when it's over. Not that you might be able to guess from the lights turning off in the theater indicates that the show is about to start. You actually need a host to inform you thusly.

I remember participating in one company celebration where there was food and games for everybody who wanted to play. In order to make it more predictable how much food of every type was needed every participant got vouchers in the beginning to make sure that everybody could enjoy any of these dishes only once. For example there was an electric bull riding game which you just could play if you had a voucher for it – the whole day I did not see anybody using it at all. But it was a great idea to give out vouchers to control the masses.

There are no limits to your creativity regarding the kind of rules you can create and how to enforce them. Since labor is not really expensive over here you might have to hire hundreds of people to make sure everybody follows your rules. And do not forget to make sure that the people you hired also follow the rules by adding another layer of watchdogs watching the watchdogs. But these also might need supervision so… get a watchdog for the watchdog for the watchdog. You get the point.

10 Study/Work Hard (Or Know How to Cheat)!

One of the first big challenges everybody has to face on the way of becoming an adult is the so called "Gao Kao", a test in which you have to prove that you are qualified enough to go to university. The higher your score in it is the better the university you can go to.

Since parents really want you to go to a good university there is lots of pressure on the children, but also much support in many ways, e.g. they run around the test buildings to keep these noisy birds away, which could disturb concentration. For the ones who did not prepare themselves in order to do well on the Gao Kao there are plenty of ways to cheat. But be aware that nobody catches you – cheating at Gao Kao is quite an offense and you should not get caught while doing so.

After finishing the Gao Kao you will have an easy way in ahead of you – if you passed that one and you were able to go to university you will surely finish up your studies there successfully. Since I was teaching at a university here once I have some experience in identifying cheaters: In one of the tests I had to pull a new cheater out of the test every 3 minutes – meaning three hours into the test there weren't many students left who returned the finished paper test to me. And yes, the cheaters complained a lot.

I never had the great opportunity to study here for a degree but at least the grading scheme while studying Chinese at university was pretty amazing.

Task: Make a presentation about some kind of food in your country in Chinese.

Grading:

- 30% If you did a presentation in PowerPoint
- 50% if you hold the presentation, not caring about quality

So if you just did these two things, you already got 80% of the score with the final 20% being judging the quality.

Did I mention already that with over 90% you are considered being an "outstanding" student?

If you look at the mess at the education system where everybody is drilled to memorize things, beginning from the Chinese characters up to complete English lectures – and yes, just memorizing all the lesson does not help you to hold a conversation in English – it is no surprise that people will often do something completely different in their jobs than their majors at university. It does not really matter WHAT you studied, it matters at WHICH UNIVERSITY you studied to find a good job later. It is completely natural to meet people who studied English for years and still can tell you a lesson word by word, but are not able to say a sentence they did not memorize.

Except for the Gao Kao there is not much where you really have to be a hard worker – it is much more important that you spend endless hours in the process, it doesn't matter how much you really do during that time. Efficiency is unnecessary. You will meet many people here that will work 6 days a week (or more) and 12 hours a day (or more). Without being too mean to some people who really work hard, "working" mostly means you are present at work. But you should really look around in some of these offices, e.g. real estate rental agencies, to see what they mean by "working": Surfing the internet, sleeping on the desk, talking to colleagues, or having a smoke. You can do whatever you want, just be physically present. This will also influence the days of vacation you will have: Many companies do not give out more than five days of vacation a year. Get used to this, especially if you are working at an "iron rice bowl" – a state owned company which surely will not be known for its efficiency but for the stability of the jobs there.

Since companies are promoting "lifelong learning" in Europe quite a lot lately this is a concept that you will find here pretty soon: Especially when you are younger you should do what the Chinese do and change your jobs often. As soon as you understood your job and are good at it – change it. Because you want to learn more and increase your salary it is also very common to do job-hopping.

11 Rest Even Harder!

Resting even harder is totally true in two ways: Literally and not so literally. Let's have a look at the not so literal way first: When you are in this amazing country you will see a lot of people sleeping everywhere. I especially love the view of security guards falling asleep on duty. Presence is everything, and well, who would be scared of these slender and untrained/unfit security guards anyway. If you have some other profession do not be afraid, there are plenty of other choices: On the grass, on the desk in the office, under the desk, in the warehouse of your company, hidden behind some boxes, in the car or bus which is especially true for drivers waiting for their guests. As a guest on a taxi stuck in traffic jam you can also take a nap, or the driver takes a nap while taking a break to prevent to be stuck in traffic jam.

The perfect resting plan also should observe the actual weather conditions. If it is too hot stay at home and rest. If it is too cold stay at home and rest. If it is raining stay at home and rest. You get the point. You should probably stay at home all the time anyway. And rest.

After a long day of working, studying, or even resting there is one more thing that you should never forget in order to stay healthy: Go to bed early. Going out too late or returning home too late is neither traditional nor healthy or any other way of well accepted behavior so go home early. If you do not care about that you can be pretty sure that – depending on your own age and living circumstances –

somebody else will. University dormitories usually close and lock up at some point in time, and if you are still living at home your parents might call you and ask about your whereabouts. If you do not have the time to return home during the day for a good nap it doesn't matter – get comfortable wherever you are. In the office you can rest your head on your desk while the better prepared ones have a cushion there already anyway. If you ask around a bit what people do here as a hobby you might hear "sleeping" pretty often. This is hard to miss in everyday life.

Now to the more literal way: I will talk about being healthy the Chinese way in another chapter, but you will surely have some back-breaking experiences with Chinese mattresses. If you ever tried to sleep on a wooden floor you might recognize this feeling of pain the next day, obviously depending on whether or not you managed to fall asleep at all. Since Chinese people believe that a hard mattress is good for the back – this might even be true – it might be a killer for your back in the beginning. At least for mine it was and sometimes it still is. My personal solution was not buying a new mattress, which can easily be as expensive as my apartment for a whole month, but buying an "add-on" – a really soft and still not that thick foam shaped like my mattress to rid me of the feeling of sleeping on rocks.

If you want to push the quality of your sleep even further you can also go to a furniture store and snore in the demonstration beds. It is really fun to walk through a famous Swedish furniture brand store in Beijing and watch the people snoring in beds, having a good rest. But before buying a new mattress – you really should try it out first, right?

Thus, if you really want to be a Chinese you should rest even harder. Pun totally intended.

12   Take Care of Your Health!

In a country that is plagued with bad pollution it is really important that you take care of your health. There are some basic rules that you should follow to be a true Chinese health keeper: Drink hot water. Listen to the body temperature. Eat the right food for your condition. If something is wrong take some Traditional Chinese Medicine (TCM).

In my opinion there might be historical reasons why Chinese people love hot or at least warm water. If you knew that water out of the sink was pretty poisonous you would also get used to the taste and habit of drinking hot water. But whatever might be wrong with your body drinking hot water is THE solution. You have a headache? Drink more hot water. In the summer the temperature is over 30 degrees and you are sweating? Drink more hot water. You have any other problem with your body? Drink more hot water. These are the recommendations that you will hear a lot whatever is wrong with you. If you consider that the whole nation is drinking hot water all day, only sometimes with added taste by tea leafs, you might be wondering how anyone could ever get sick here. And even if you do not drink hot water then your drinks should at least be room temperature. But even I have to admit that times are changing - if you order a "cold beer" you will mostly not end up with beer and ice cubes anymore. But it still might happen occasionally.

Listening to the body temperature - mostly diagnosed by a doctor of traditional Chinese medicine, sometimes diagnosed by you or your colleagues - is also really helpful in planning the food and drinks you can consume. If your facial skin is not well maybe it's because your body is producing too much heat. If your teeth are hurting bad then your body is also producing too much heat. Going to a dentist is totally overrated. Depending whether or not your body is producing too much heat you should choose your diet accordingly, e.g. you should not eat anything spicy anymore. If you are a girl on your period, yes, your body is producing too much heat. You should not eat any ice cream. Instead, drink more hot water.

Eating the right dish for your condition might be really a bit hard to understand if you are not a doctor in Traditional Chinese Medicine yet. I'll just give you a hint: follow the recommendations of your Chinese colleagues. If they tell you that something is "good for men", then it increases your potency. If some kind of soup is very "nutritious" then you should drink it. If it tastes weird but your friends tell you it is good for your health - eat it.

While this Traditional Chinese Medicine plays such a big role in life there is no better way to show off than showing everybody pictures of your hand with an infusion needle on the social media website of your preference. And you will get a lot of infusions since this is the standard treatment in the hospital for basically everything obviously. Another issue on the health side is sports: You really should start playing Ping Pong and/or Badminton. I barely know any Chinese who cannot play at least one of these two sports. More and more popular is the gym which is always an experience in itself – depending on the price level you can expect a high class gym including steam room and luxurious changing rooms, but mostly you will be scared to touch the floor with your feet in the changing room, so bring your own slippers. And if you are used to disinfectants in your home country to disinfect the sporting machines before and after your training you should not expect anything as luxurious here. For the older generation next to dancing on the street you always have the option to use one of the free public gyms in parks to keep your body in shape.

You should never underestimate how important a good night's sleep is, and never ever forget: Drink hot water first.

13 Get a Red Stamp, Lots of Documents and FaPiaos

Even before arriving here in this amazing country I ran into the "red stamp" already: For getting a student visa you will need a physical exam. On the internet I found the very useful hint that it should be stamped with a red stamp – with this color it is much more likely to be accepted by the Chinese authorities. Just a side note: You cannot imagine how hard it is to find a doctor willing to do the physical exam and to stamp it in red color afterwards.

If you open your eyes a bit you will find that Chinese people really love to chop everything that looks official. And while in western companies documents are usually signed by the Managing Director or somebody authorized by him, here in China it is usually the person who has the red company chop under control, but sometimes there are additional signatures required. If you plan to start a company here please be careful about this company chop, otherwise you might have stamped contracts in the end that were never supposed to be stamped. To make it even more complicated you can find various kinds of chops: Next to the company chop there is a financial chop, a contract chop, a customs chop, an invoice chop, and more. To make it even more confusing there is a stamping tax that has to be paid.

As you might have recognized already it is impossible to stamp anything digital, you need paper to stamp yourself out. While in the western world companies are trying to make the processes as digital as possible you might get the impression here that companies try to produce as many paper forms as possible. I highly recommend going to the bank to open an account there: You will fill out several forms, everything will be stamped, maybe even twice or three times. You check in to a hotel? Never lose the stamped papers that prove you've made a deposit.

I also remember the process of how to play badminton at my university:

Step number 1: Get a reservation for the field on a stamped piece of paper.

Step number 2: On the designated date go to the reception, give them the stamped piece of paper and you get a new (stamped) piece of paper.

Step number 3: With that piece of paper go to the court where you will get another piece of paper in exchange, sadly this time without a stamp.

To make it short: for every possible circumstance you will get so many paper documents you will easily get lost. If your Chinese is not that amazing yet you should make small notes on the paper to remember afterwards what it is for.

One special document you might encounter a lot is the so called "FaPiao" – basically an invoice with special features. You might have guessed it: It has a stamp or at least a print of a stamp on it. Be aware that you can always try to bargain down the price of food in a restaurant if you tell them that you do not need a FaPiao. Of course the process behind these FaPiaos is a bit more complicated than it seems: They have to be bought by the shop at the tax authorities. Businesses do not have a legal obligation to give you one, but as a customer you can always ask for one. And if you are lucky in the end the shop still has some FaPiaos on stock. If not they might either offer you a discount or send the FaPiao to you by post afterwards – or you can pick it up few days later by yourself.

Since the Chinese government does not really trust the inhabitants of this country to pay taxes by free will they invented the "FaPiao lottery": On some of the FaPiaos there is a scratch field where you can use a coin to find out whether you won money or whether the Chinese government simply says "Thanks" for making sure that it receives taxes.

To help you to become a real Chinese I will come back to my health certificate problem in the beginning. The solution was to bring the red colored ink pad to the doctor myself and convince him to use it otherwise I would go to another doctor. This was basically a bluff since most of the other doctors already told me they will not chop anything in red.

Since I got this health certificate in another country I was sadly not able to get a FaPiao or ask the doctor for a discount.

14 Pay Upfront and Never Forget the Deposit!

When you arrive you will make a discovery quite soon: You probably need more money than you expected in the beginning. And you will probably leave the country with more local currency than you wanted to. For many services you will have to pay upfront plus a deposit – this way you will mostly know that you won't have to pay more money for a service until your upfront payment runs out.

When entering a hotel you are expected to pay the nights you want to stay in advance when checking in, and the deposit varies a lot but is usually around the room rate for one night. This also applies if there is no minibar – so it might be a bit confusing what the deposit is for. Maybe if someone destroys all the appliances they would keep the deposit but I've always gotten it back. And on a side note be advised that Chinese hotel rooms usually come equipped with shower gel, toothbrush and toothpaste and depending on the price level also with other features like body lotion. When I was travelling to China only once a year for vacation it became kind of a habit to spend all my money and use the money from the deposit to pay for the taxi back to the airport.

It might be a little bit more complicated if you decide to rent an apartment: You usually pay the rent for three months in cash, depending on local regulations, and in case a real estate agency was involved one month worth of rent to them, and also one month worth of rent as security deposit for the landlord. Either make sure your credit card limit is high enough to pick up this money within one day or plan ahead accordingly. Even when you have to pay the next three months later be prepared to do it either in cash or run to the ATM, pick up some cash then use an ATM of your landlord's bank to make a deposit into their account again. Sounds complicated but it's probably much easier than hassling around with bank transfers here.

You might find other opportunities to make deposits and/or upfront payments in other places as well: Some restaurants do it, car rental agencies do it, mobile phone cards often work on a prepaid basis, and even water and electricity have to be paid beforehand. Sometimes with the amazing effect that either water or electricity run out while you are in the shower, in the dark and/or fully soaped up without any way to wash it off. In this case all you can do is to hope that the office where you can recharge your prepaid card is still open and not too far away – walk there, recharge, and insert the card in the corresponding slot in your apartment. Sounds simple but can get on your nerves. Just be sure that you never run out of cash or low on your prepaid card (for whatever it may be) or you might run out of money in the worst situation you can imagine. And always be aware of your limit on the credit card if you do not have enough cash here.

15 Go Shopping

If you ask around what your other Chinese companions did last weekend you will find out that shopping might be somewhere on the top of the list – somewhere next to resting, sleeping, and eating some amazing food.

Due to the big progress in Chinese society you can choose the shopping experience that most fits your needs. Let's begin with the luxury shopping: Is China known as the country of fake brands in your country? Well, this is true. But people who have money to spare – and even the ones who don't – will surely go for true luxury. From the small scale, e.g. the very popular electronic products made by a company with a fruity logo to the very large scale including expensive watches, suitcases, cars, and whatever this world might offer. In foreign countries Chinese tourists are more and more welcome since they maybe book cheap tours but will spend lots and lots of money on their trips shopping. I have never heard about a special expensive brand of suitcases until I met Chinese travel groups in my hometown. After one third of the travel group bought this suitcase, because with a price tag of 600 Euro each it was considered cheap, I couldn't help but to remember that brand forever. They didn't do anything in this town (which really has some very nice places to offer) except go for lunch, go shopping in special shops that cater specifically to Chinese citizens, including a Chinese shopkeeper, Chinese signs, and of course accepting Chinese bank cards. Not only abroad Chinese people can get crazy about luxury

– even the nice and historical area around the drum and bell tower in Beijing will be converted into a shopping area for expensive watches. Goodbye history and unique area, hello money spenders. And yes, you will probably not meet too many Chinese people in the fake-markets with fake brands.

If you do not have that much to spare you can also just walk along the street and have a look at the many smaller shopping malls where you can either do cheap no-name shopping, only sometimes encountering a bad fake of a popular brand, or the a little bit more expensive places which look like western malls. If you are really tired of visiting malls there are plenty of opportunities on the street where people are selling bags, clothes, cups, earphones, protection layers for your smartphone, fruits, makeup, shoes, … whatever you are looking for simply walk along the streets for long enough and you will find somebody selling these things. And while you're at it be a bit confused that many smaller shops selling more or less exactly the same have a tendency to be all located in one area. Whenever you need to buy a new tire for your car the next shop might be far away. But if you find a shop selling these you can be sure there will be more neighboring it.

Last but not least you can also spend your money online which might be a bit complicated for a foreigner not speaking Chinese – you will either not find what you are looking for or you might not be able to pay with your credit card. Even if you somehow succeed to buy something online at a shop you might have trouble understanding the packet delivery guy who will always give you a call on the way to check if you really are at home. But if you navigate around these issues somehow you will find a world full of cheap products, sometimes very good quality, and delivery within just a few hours. Did you ever try to buy something in the morning in your own country to be delivered in the afternoon? This might happen here since logistics are truly amazing.

Anyway, shopping can be a big part of your life here. And whatever you start to enjoy in this process – looking for something, negotiating a price, opening the package as soon as it has arrived, or even the shouting at the delivery guy on the phone because you do not understand a word. As a true Chinese shopping should be a big part of your life from now on.

16 Learn About "Face" and Guangxi

If you read the topic closely you will realize this is basically for your understanding of these topics and not that much about specific rules to follow. This would fill books on its own and there would still be people around who would have a different opinion on these aspects. And in my opinion as a foreigner there is not really much you can or have to do about this. But no book about Chinese culture would be complete without these topics – if you are a more or less considerate person you should be fine with this. I just wanted to mention it.

Let us start with "Guangxi": It is said that in China you will need "Guangxi", meaning more or less relationships with people or a personal network, in order to be successful. It is all about networks which will help you in business or private life. The good news (or bad news) is: You can forget about this completely because you will never be able to establish a really good network anyway. Most of these networks are tied because of family matters or after having spent years together, e.g. going to school and studying together afterwards. Of course it is also possible to establish a network by participating in the drinking ritual, but they will never be as strong as the ones developed over long periods of time. And even if you do somehow manage to stablish a personal network it will never be extremely reliable as a foreigner. I have met many, many foreigners coming here who thought that they have good connections – and most of them were pulled back to the harsh reality as soon as they needed something from this network. Small favors can be done, big favors mostly not. Establishing a good network depends on lots of trust, which doesn't happen within one semester of staying here to study a bit of Chinese or by working here for a year. But how is this different from your own country? If you look really closely at your friendships I guess that most of your best friends are the really old ones.

Next to "Guangxi" the next, in my humble opinion totally overly exaggerated aspect is the concept of "face". You should not lose face. You should give others face. But ask around, what the heck is face? Well, in my opinion it is this: Be nice to others, support them, and speak in a good way of them in front of others. Do not criticize them in front of others and take care that you do not embarrass them in front of others. That's it.

Sounds simple? It actually is. If you are not a totally stupid idiot with no idea how to behave around other people just behave a little bit better and you will be fine.

Even if you read this guide over and over again and internalized every aspect everybody will still easily see that you are a foreigner and they will forgive you minor flaws. Just don't be the stereotypic yet sadly existing language teacher who came to this country without any knowledge about anything except his or her own language, feeling like a god because everybody is so nice to them. You should never forget that you are a guest in this amazing country – even if everybody is nice to you it doesn't mean that you are in any way better. It simply means this is part of the culture and you should adapt to it by being nice to others, too. After you've had your first experience of trying to calm down a drunken and angry 50-kg-girl trying to push her out the door of a bar because she's starting to smash glasses and insulting random people in there out of frustration you will realize that this entire concept of losing face is totally overrated in many books about Chinese culture.

Still there is something you can do to make yourself a bit more popular: Play the status game. There are plenty of ways to make someone else feel important and good – and even if you probably never learn all of the ways how to show somebody respect there are some simple ways to do it.

Once again let's take one of the most common activities you might join here: Eating and drinking, where you can really live it out.

You should probably get a Chinese advisor anyway in case you're having dinner with an important person, but at least two rules are pretty easy to remember: The most important person is placed facing the door. This way he does not have to turn around each time somebody is entering the room and the servants do not get in his way too often. Left and right of him are the next ones on the important-list, and so on. The poor guy sitting with the back to the door is considered the least important person and probably will end up paying the bill. Ah, the bill… another important thing: Stop being greedy and fight about paying the bill in the end to show the others how important they are to you. While sitting there and – yes, you remember that chapter probably – drinking alcohol you might be required clink your glasses with somebody else. Make it a habit to lower your glass a bit to show the other one how great his status is compared to yours. If he also knows this rule, this might result in him lowering the glass, too. If you continue this long enough, you both will at some point reach the floor and clink the glasses there. This is always good for a laugh. To prevent this you can also practice to get your glass closer to the one of the other person on one level, then suddenly lower it before the two glasses meet.

When you've finished your drink you should also be polite enough to refill his glass –first help the others before you fill up your own glass. And if somebody else was quicker than you then at least tap your fingers next to the glass a couple of times to show your appreciation.

If you are in a lucky enough position to be a high guest with somebody serving you around be sure not to do too much yourself. Let somebody else carry your luggage, throw your garbage anywhere and let somebody else clean up, let somebody else deal with all the small troubles life might bring to you. This is what they are getting paid for probably.

Sometimes you still consider yourself being a very important person but there is nobody around who can show all the people. In this case you can simply bring along expensive things to impress everybody or participate in activities that might be too expensive for the average Chinese to participate: Buy a luxury car, if available it should be in a long version, maybe an SUV where you can sit in a higher position and look down at everybody with a car cheaper than yours. Bring along expensive watches, clothes, shoes, and accessories that might impress everybody around. If the usual things are not enough to impress anyone you can buy new phones of the brand with a fruity logo before they are officially available in China to give them to all the children in your son's class as a present. Some other guy also bought 99 of these phones to use them in a confession of love to his girlfriend – and please be reminded that the price for a single one of these phones is probably at least 1.5 times the average salary here. Maybe this will give an outlook on how much the wedding will cost...

My task for you to become Chinese in this chapter is pretty easy: Show others how much you value them if you consider them important. Play the status game. Show others that they should value you. Let them play the status game. For me this is much easier if I take it as a fun challenge – and not being serious about it: It can actually be fun as long as I do not have to buy too many new phones…

Do not forget what is considered a good treat in your own culture. Add a bit more to the "be good to other people" side, do not forget that these things exist in your own culture as well – and then simply live it. Before you say or do anything think about how it might make the other person feel. And if you are not a total sociopath I guess you do not want to make other people feel bad. Treat them the way you want to be treated, only better.

17   Bend the Truth and Play the Blame Game

Sometimes it is funny; sometimes it is so frustrating that you want to hit your head against the wall: The blame game. Nobody wants to be responsible for anything so if something goes wrong everybody is trying to find somebody else to blame. Yeah, sure, I have seen that in western countries, too. But I have never seen anything to an extent like here. You want some examples? Here we go: As we all know China is facing some serious environmental problems– the most visible one being air pollution, but also water and soil not being the healthiest ones. But thank god that we have smart government officials who found somebody to blame: It must be the barbecue restaurants on the streets that use charcoal to prepare their meat sticks. To fight the pollution he honestly suggested closing down all of these restaurants – because their influence on air quality of course is much bigger than the millions of cars and factories or the missing enforcement of any environmental protection rules. At some point another government official obviously thought that this idea with the BBQ might not be right, and he had a different yet also great idea, since everybody here is so fixed about eating. He found a new origin of the pollution: It must be the cigarette smokers that cause these problems. So he wanted to ban cigarettes. I guess his opinion will not be shared by most of the government officials since the heaviest smokers are probably government officials themselves.

This leads to the next conclusion: The government is to blame for the pollution. Or the factories. Or the cars. It is especially fun to listen to this when somebody is getting out of his oversized SUV and complaining about the air here, but obviously showing off is much more important than taking a bit of self-responsibility.

This is not only the case with air but also true for any other kind of trash: People throw their trash everywhere. From cigarette stumps to empty bottles to everything else, just drop it like it's hot – and afterwards complain about the pollution. Whoever's fault it is, maybe the cleaning workers', the government's, or somebody else's, it surely cannot be yours.

Since it will always be recognizable that you are not Chinese please bear in mind that you should not criticize the government as a foreigner. While everywhere on earth people might not be really happy if you say something bad about the social group they belong too here you might quickly end your conversations if you do this. Play the blame game but never blame anyone around you at that time or anyone in any connection to the person you are talking to when blaming somebody. Criticism from inside a social group is not really open but might be accepted. Criticism from the outside will quickly be labeled as foreign propaganda.

18   Be Racist

Raised in a culture where you are always told how bad racism is and where everybody with racist behavior is considered to be of the rather uneducated kind this might be the hardest chapter for me to write about. I need to mention once again that this is not how I am or want to be but one of the big, hard steps you have to take to become truly Chinese is being racist, which can be divided into two different kinds of racism: Positive racism and negative racism, depending on your skin color – this might not be such a big surprise.

The average white foreigner will be treated friendly and nice, mostly much friendlier than a local can expect to be treated. This does not mean that the people here will change 100 percent from being selfish but at least most people here will treat you nicer than they would treat locals. It starts with the small things – if you ask for something they might be much friendlier with you, but it goes far deeper: Depending on the city you are at you will be invited for drinks in bars (which is not that common anymore in first tier cities but very much so everywhere else), people want to be friends with you very quickly and you sometimes get preferred treatment because you are white. There are also professions called "face jobs" where you are exclusively being paid for being white. Some companies employ foreigners just to show that they have the money and reputation to do this. And if you do not want to really work there for a long time you can do this also on a time basis: You will get some fake name cards and will be sent to exhibitions to show how international the exhibition is. You will be invited to customer events and introduced there as some kind of European or American business partner and participate in the drinking rituals there or hold a speech in your own language, while somebody "translates" into whatever they really want you to say. The less Mandarin you speak the better.

This also goes for TV shows where foreigners are sometimes invited, or even English teaching jobs where sometimes the real qualification is not that important as long as you have a white face. The other gender will immediately give you more attention because you are foreign. Being white is something good here. It does not matter how much you try, your face will always be foreign so be prepared to hear a lot of people mentioning that there is a foreigner walking around ("Laowai!") or people whispering "hello" when you cross them.

If there is a bright side about white foreigners there must also be a "black" and dark side. Being dark-skinned is here not considered a good thing for the Chinese people already, but being black is even worse: The people here think that black people are dirty and stink or they often are considered to be criminals and violent. And many people do not want to get too close with black people. It might also be hard for you to score a "face job" or even a job as English teacher here, even if your language and teaching skills are actually really good.

Even worse off than the dark colored people are people from Japan. Sure, China and Japan do not share a friendly history which should not be discussed here – but if you see a big sign at a club saying that "dog and Japanese are not allowed to enter", including a big picture of Chinese victims who were tortured to death, you should not be surprised.

Last but not least, China is an amazingly big country and it is no surprise that there are some superstitions regarding other minorities – especially people from Xinjiang are often considered to be thieves or criminals of any kind. People in Beijing think that the people from Shanghai are greedy. And so on.

As I've mentioned I was raised in a culture nurturing an open society without racism, so I do not want to give you any clues as to how to be more racist. And even if this might be a big requirement for you to master the Chinese culture go and figure it out yourself. Or try to be a "better" Chinese than most of the people here and forget about being racist.

19 Get Loud and Let Others Enjoy the Sounds, Smells and Fluids Your Body Can Produce

The Chinese translation for "lively" is a mix between the words for "hot" and "make noise" – and this is literally how life is lived here. This is definitely no quiet country: Walking along the shopping streets you will have lots of people shouting advertisements at you or just playing music as loud as in an average music club. When trucks or small cars are in reverse they sometimes make beeping noises or shout "take care about safety" every few seconds to warn people behind. Same thing with escalators in subway stations, where you are reminded to "stand firm and hold the handrail". In restaurants people sometimes talk so loud that you get the feeling they are fighting with each other until they suddenly burst out in laughter. Bars might be quiet in the beginning but no matter how many people are in there it gets louder every half an hour in the evening so it is almost impossible to talk to each other after 10 p.m. – and nightclubs, well, they are that loud to begin with already. If you're worried about your ears you should bring along earplugs. Having a conversation can be impossible there but do not fear – communication is still possible by playing drinking games since you can get dices everywhere, or simply by using your phone which can be seen quite often in nightclubs, too.

Since you are part of this exciting atmosphere all the time it is no big wonder that you barely meet Chinese people who are able to whisper or talk quietly no matter what the situation. The closest thing to whispering is somebody holding his hand in front of his mouth while talking to you. You want to make yourself heard. But this is only true for people speaking their own language: I've met so many people who really have loud and aggressive voices while speaking Mandarin but as soon as they switch their language to another one their voice suddenly becomes soft and sounds a bit insecure, much like that of a young child.

Your body is an amazing tool to contribute to this lively atmosphere. Contrary to popular opinion in other countries your bodily fluids, sounds, and smells are enrichment to the environment. One of the things you will pretty quickly discover is that people enjoy spitting, sometimes accompanied with the deep grunting noise to pull up as much slime as possible from very deep places within your body. Disgusting? You will get used to it, especially after you start doing it yourself. Obviously the massive marketing campaigns trying to get people to be more civilized and stop spitting everywhere are not really working that well yet.

Public vomiting is also quite a sport here. Just imagine for a second somebody vomiting in the yard of your favorite restaurant - I guess the waiters would not be very happy. Here, it is amazingly common for somebody to be that drunk that he vomits where he is sitting, while somebody else is padding them on the back comforting them while continuing to eat with a big smile. And as soon as the vomiting procedure is over there is enough space in the stomach that the person can drink more alcohol again.

After you got used to all the spitting and vomiting by doing it yourself (which is amazingly fun) your next task is not to care about the smell that your body produces after having great food. There is nothing better than eating lots and lots of garlic – and meeting your boyfriend/girlfriend afterwards. On my way to the first blind date with a girl, do you know how I could locate which one it is in the café? I just followed the smell. Even three meters away you could smell it, imagine how fun it is to be sitting in front of her. Sometimes the smell might be not that bad but imagine you want to kiss a cute girl and suddenly you realize that she obviously ate a whole bowl of garlic for breakfast. Outside of dating, there are many other opportunities where you will have breath-taking experiences: On the subway, in the taxi, in the office, or on the street. Basically anywhere: Sometimes in a good way but mostly it is quite disturbing. Either way it's a world full of smells, sometimes produced by the body and sometimes by something else like a kitchen below your hotel room.

And last but not least you should enjoy the sounds that your body can produce. Especially while eating you should eat as loud as possible - make slurping noises while pulling the long noodles into your mouth or while drinking the soup. Somehow practical, because this way it is a little bit less likely that your shirt will get dirty while eating, somehow for the better taste. This is at least what people say here. But especially you should do it for fun.

Public farting is maybe not that common but burping can be heard sometimes. Is there anything sexier than a girl burping just before you kiss her? Or clearing the throat of the slime while being in a kissing session? If you think that this is unsexy, well, you haven't been here long enough yet. And well, Chinese girls… if you listen closely to all the sounds in the hallway of a Chinese hotel you might hear a girl shouting and moaning as if she was in a porn movie (which is of course forbidden to buy and watch here).

My suggestion for you is this: Remember what your parents told you about bad behavior. Write it down. And make it a To-Do-List of the things that you should do instead of not doing it. Start burping, yawning or sneezing without covering your mouth with your hand, vomiting, peeing and eating smelly food before going on a date. Who cares, anyway?

20   Travel the Chinese Way

While welfare is becoming increasingly, more and more tourists are traveling around as well – inside and outside of the country. But wherever you meet Chinese travel groups you will see somebody leading the group with a small flag or something else that is easy to be spotted. Nobody should get lost. After traveling for a while with Chinese groups, you will definitely have the urge to follow every small flag around.

Individual travel is becoming more and more popular, however, but when you look at the average travel group you will unmistakably be under the impression that this is a kindergarten on tour. Let us just have a brief look on any random tourist site here: If there is something made by nature or something historic, most of the other countries would probably try to preserve it more or less. Here, it is a bit different: The first thing that is going to happen is that somebody will put up a big entrance gate where you have to spend an awful lot of money after fighting yourself through the line to get an entrance ticket. Once you are inside you will of course have the attraction itself. But next to it you will always find a spot where you can dress up in "traditional" clothes of that or any other region to get some pictures taken. Some souvenir shops in the weirdest places. No place is already beautiful enough that it cannot be pimped. Natural caves, which took millions of years to develop the way they are right now, will get a light and sound show inside – and of course the switch for it will be more or less drilled in a stalactite while the lights are put into the floor and ceiling. Then you might have to pay something extra for a side-cave where you can donate to the turtle king, turtle queen, turtle mistress, and turtle-whatever to get really lucky. In villages where you can take a look at how the "old tribes" used to live there will be at least one crazy show which makes you feel like you're in Disneyland, only much worse. Next to an amazing lake in the middle of the desert they started building a race track for karts. On the beach you might find small tanks with electric engines with which you can drive your children around playing war during the day and weird shows including fire you can participate in at night, right after singing Karaoke directly on the sand of the beach. In a snow village you have to pay extra to see a part from outside where it is forbidden to go in to enjoy the big layers of snow on the top of some buildings.

Even once spiritual places like temples are money machines now: During my travels I've seen a fortune teller that definitely belonged to the temple several times who wanted to tell me my future for free. After agreeing, he found out that something horrible will happen to me, but thank god he can help me if I donate a lot of money. If I donate even more money I will be lucky in the future. Yeah, sure. Some people might believe it the first time but if that happens to you with every fortune teller you run into it really makes it much less believable.

And even old stories are used to squeeze money out of tourists: In one temple it is said that if you steal some small toy there you will have lucky children. Thus, for a "small donation" the monk will put a small toy on the table and turn around so you can steal it. Awesome.

It is also possible to have fun for free – ask some random strangers, especially foreigners, if they can take pictures with you. Most of them are used to Chinese people doing that anyway – it happens quite a lot to foreigners that random locals just ask you if you can take a picture with them. You should join this custom and also ask people you do not know for a group picture. I guess their reaction when a non-Chinese will ask them is pretty priceless.

When traveling abroad, tourist groups or groups of business people (there is not much difference sometimes) will have some kind of vacation package including flights, transfer, hotels and organized meals. And every day there is at least ONE Chinese meal, otherwise the poor travelers would totally die of hunger since they are not the biggest fans of western food anyway, even if they try to pimp it with garlic and soy sauce that they brought along. In between these meals the poor tour guide has to make sure that nobody gets lost by shouting directions, raising the flag, and giving the lost people phone calls every few minutes. And how are these tour guides qualified to do their job? No idea, some of them do not even speak the local language or English. But most of the tourists also do not really care about the sightseeing attractions since the most important thing they will do is shopping everywhere, anyway.

Since you now know how Chinese traveling works you should really join the fun. Follow the small flags. Drive your tour guide crazy by not listening and wandering off. Feel back to the time when you were a child in kindergarten and go nuts. You'll love it – and even if you do not, you will love watching others doing it.

21   Get a Chinese Name

I guess I could continue writing for ages of small stories what you should do here and what not. But I guess a big step for you on your long journey of becoming Chinese is getting a Chinese name. And for this you should really get a consultant. You might recognize that this country seems more bilingual than it really is: Almost everybody has some kind of English first name. Sometimes a pretty common name like Julia, sometimes the name is a bit weird like Honey or Rainbow. But my personal favorite is somebody called Smacker.

Since it is either modern to have an English name or all of these people want to make it easier for you to remember theirs, you should really find a Chinese name. This is not only out of courtesy, at least if you want to stay here longer you will need one, e.g. to get the working permit. Sometimes even for small things like the "Deep Water Swimming Qualification license", where I had to show some guy for about 10 minutes that I can swim in order to be allowed to go to the deep side of the swimming pool. This license comes fully equipped with a passport picture and a Chinese name, because – you guessed it – you have to make sure that nobody pretends with my license that he can swim and then drowns because his swimming capabilities are as developed as the ones of a stone. Even for some bigger things, like a driving license, you will need a Chinese name.

While it is always a pleasure to read the menus in restaurants here, where you will find really weird translations, more and more places also have English names. Sometimes maybe not the best one: For example the "foot massage museum" had some mistranslation or the restaurant called "the new concept of self-care seafood barbecue Shabu" maybe was not the luckiest translation, either. So you better find somebody who knows local culture and can give you a good name. You do not want to make the mistake of translating your name just by exchanging your letters through syllables that sound a bit like your name in your own language. Otherwise you might also translate "Facebook" with "Feisibuke": This basically means you "are condemned to die". Or a famous brand of soft drinks that first mistranslated their own company name into "mouth full with wax".

When you got your name you should remember it well – but do not mind that nobody will call you by it. If somebody is called "Dong Ge" they might just call you "Xiao Ge" or "Da Ge", which just means "big or small Ge", depending on their relative age to yours.

Talking about family names – since there are more Mr. Wang or Mr. Li than most of the countries have as total population, it might be a big wonder for you how they distinguish each other. This is not really a problem, since people mostly will not be addressed with their name but more with their title: If you spend some days with a Chinese family you will quickly be addressed as the "big" or "small" brother/sister while you can address everybody else with uncle and auntie. Sounds easy in English, but it is not in Chinese – since there is not only one word for aunt but depending if the aunt is the sister of the mother or the father there are other words for it. Thus, simply explaining the relationships in your close family to anyone will require an awesome Chinese skill. Also, at work people will be addressed as "Manager Wang", "Secretary Li" or anything like that. But what happens if there are several "Manager Wang" in a company? How do you distinguish them? To be honest, I have no idea. This is the best time for you to fall back to English names again. There are probably not many people called "Angel Wang" in your company. And since Chinese names might be pretty confusing to you anyway you can also start to copy Chinese people and mix up "he" and "she" regularly – which somehow comes as a surprise to me, since at least in the written form there is also a separation of the two genders in mandarin.

22 Get a Chinese Quality Room

The Great Wall of China has been there for thousands of years. The Forbidden City has been around for hundreds of years. They were built to last and even while there have been renovations in parts, they are solid. Yet somehow the art of building quality houses was lost afterwards. You will be amazed how the skyscrapers are growing here: While the construction industry is building new houses (including ghost towns) like crazy it is more about the quantity then the quality. Sad thing is: It does not really take long until they are pretty much run down. And sometimes the construction projects even run out of money before they finish: If you walk around a bit with open eyes you will see plenty of buildings that are half-finished for years without any progress. One of my favorite examples is Wonderworld near Beijing where they started to build an amusement park, including entrance gates, a restaurant street, and a nice castle in the middle. Suddenly, they stopped due to lack of funding, and since there was no progress in construction anymore the farmers returned to grow their corn there. Construction abandoned.

Even if they somehow manage to finish the construction quality will probably not be comparable to the western world: While the buildings might even have small problems in the beginning already they will get worse pretty quickly. I moved into an apartment complex that was not even finished yet, and all my water outlets were already leaking: the toilet, the water heater for the shower, etc. After calling the janitors they had a brief look, discovered that they have no idea, and will leave it as is.

Since Beijing can become pretty hot in summer and pretty cold in winter, isolation might be another issue that you will miss here a lot. During summer my home always feels like a Sauna and during winter like a freezer, if I do not use the air conditioning. Winter has another specialty: Most of the southern homes do not have any heating at all except air conditioning while the northern houses are mostly connected to the central heating system provided by the local government. Heating in winter? Nice. But since it is provided by the local authorities it doesn't really matter how warm or cold it is outside. On a specific day they decide to switch the heating on – and at some specific date they switch it off again. This has a very interesting effect: If it gets too hot in your apartment and you regulate the heaters in your own home this might have side-effects on the other radiators in your apartment or even your neighbors'. If you turn off heating in one of your rooms because it gets too warm your neighbor might complain afterwards that he has no heating at all. In my dormitory it was plainly forbidden to touch the thermostat. This just leaves another way of heat regulation in your apartment: Opening the window. Energy-efficiency is not really high valued (yet) even though most of the electrical appliances have some kind of energy efficiency label.

Most of the shopping malls, compounds and other big building will also start using some special heat isolation curtains for the entrances to keep the warm air inside and the cold air outside. Since they are not transparent it is always fun to enter a building, by using your hands to push the curtain aside and punch somebody in the face since you could not see through the curtains at all. And since they seem to be never cleaned and have a brown or olive green color they also do not really look very attractive but more like army supply leftovers.

With time going by buildings will run down pretty quick. While sleeping in a cheap and nice hotel in Shanghai every year it was easily possible to observe how the interior of the building deteriorated. The first year, everything was fine. The second year, they've had regular problems with their fresh water supply. The third year, wall mold moved in and the black spots inside the hotel became more and more while the tapestry was slowly disintegrating. And well, the fourth year, they closed down for good. The same thing might also happen to privately owned apartments easily. There is still a lot of room for surprises: While most of the apartment complexes can really look run-down from the outside, the apartments on the inside might still look amazing if the owner or the person living there takes care.

If you have some free time you should go to a rental agency, tell the people that you want to rent an apartment, and that you want to have a look at some of the available apartments. This is amazingly fun: You will get an insight into how Chinese people live, since they might show you some apartments where the former resident hasn't moved out yet. Or you will have a look at a big dump, where the former tenant just moved out and left everything the way it was. One of my biggest nightmares I have is taking a look at an apartment in which five cats enjoyed their freedom while the tenant had already left for over a month. It was as smelly as a zoo and the trash was piling up in some places that you could barely walk through – and still the apartment was more expensive than most of the apartments with the same size in Europe.

Even if you do not stay that long here in China you will have a pretty broad insight on hotels. It is totally accepted before checking in here that you have a look at the room, first. Use this chance to get some experience in relating price levels to standards – and if you see too many black spots on the wall, too many insects on the floor, or too much hair in the shower you should definitely consider raising your standards.

Even if you do find a place suitable for you right now do not expect to come back a few years later since the place might be closed. Construction speed but also demolition and reconstruction are crazy here. But, like an architect once told me: In about 30 years we will have the biggest museum of building damages in the world here since I guess they cannot rebuild everything again after 20 years.

23 Enjoy Music, TV Series about War and Horror Movies

As you might have heard intellectual property right or copyright is not really a very well implemented concept in this country. There is a myriad of websites or applications where you can download music and movies for free. I really feel sorry for the people who want to make their living with arts but there is no point to argue that this is amazingly convenient for the user. The best songs in the charts? Download them. Current TV shows from USA? You got it. No problem. Either you can find it on the internet or you can buy them on the street from a vendor who will be happy to sell you ten DVDs with sometimes crappy, sometimes great quality for the price of one movie ticket. And the vendor will even tell you beforehand how the quality is. But why paying for it if you can get it for free? Going to the cinema is still a great way here to spend your time, but you might be amazed that the prize for them is pretty much comparable to western countries. Bring some warm clothes since the air condition might be cold enough to freeze there while watching the movie.

The movie style that people prefer here might be pretty different. This may sound mean but from my experience the girls here can pay attention to a movie as much as a fly can pay attention to the place they are sitting at. If the movie is not full of action in the beginning already they will lose interest and start to play with their phone – or just leave you there sitting alone on the couch. When I was younger my parents always tried to show me "alternative" movies which will make you think about life issues — and yes, I enjoy these movies, mostly. With a Chinese girl at your side you will not even get passed the opening scene before she gets bored. If you want to really host a romantic movie evening watch a horror movie together, with lots of blood, or at least an action movie with as many gunshots and explosions as possible. This will keep her interested and make her blood flow.

Next to the American movies and TV series that are pretty popular here especially with the younger people the older ones seem to be mostly restricted to three topics — Chinese productions of TV series and movies mostly can be put into one of the following four categories: "Inspired" by a foreign production. A story about the true and big love. Military style, especially popular are stories about fighting the Japanese aggressors in some long-gone wars. Or ancient stories. And the real creative producers will put all these topics together to have a guaranteed success.

Just a side note: If you count how many Japanese people are killed in Chinese TV series about fighting them then you might wonder how the former enemy still exists. According to the series, the whole population of Japan must have died at least twice because of some superhero guerilla fighters. One of the most hilarious scenes in one of these TV series is a female hero being beaten, tied, and raped…. Until she finally starts to kill all the Japanese around as soon as she "sucked enough energy from her enemies", as somebody on the Chinese version of Twitter posted.

Since all these audiovisual productions need a soundtrack it might not really be a big surprise that a lot of the music here also has long-gone stories and love as their theme. While I really enjoy some of the songs here sometimes they are really hard to distinguish anyway. There the genres are even easier to distinguish, at least as a foreigner – it is an obvious love song or some kind of song that sounds pretty childish with lots of lyrics you can repeat or shout while somebody sings it. Whatever music they are playing – just enjoy it.

One last thing that might be a torture to your ears but is somehow deeply implemented in the local culture is Beijing Opera. This might be considered to be one of the cruelest tortures that were ever developed for the western mind. If you want to become truly Chinese you should at least get enough training to listen to Beijing opera for an entire show without getting a mental breakdown. Otherwise I would seriously recommend to avoid it under any circumstances.

24 Become a Master in Improvisation and Get Backup!

In a country in which plans and even laws change sometimes very suddenly you really should become a master of improvisation. During some of my numerous visits of international companies the managers told me that they are actually trying to use this creativity to improvise in their development processes. While in some other countries the scientific valuation of topics is considered a high art, here it is not that important to have the scientific background. Here it is much more important to simply get something working. Nobody cares about knowing why if you can skip this step and immediately find a working solution.

When I moved into my new apartment my refrigerator had a problem leading to massive discussions with my landlord. After spending money on technical service they managed to find out that they have no clue why the inside temperature is always about minus ten degrees and everything freezes inside, which by the way was considered perfectly normal by my landlord. Since the landlord was fed up with spending money on technical service, she sent me an electronic time switch which seems to be specifically designed for this kind of challenge. Well, the freezer still has that problem, but since the electronic time switch switches electricity on and off every 20 minutes, the temperature inside in average is now a smooth 5 degree and I do not have to be frustrated about all my frozen drinks and food.

Other repairs are also carried out as quickly as possible yet sometimes the people do not really consider the long-lasting effects: Managing a problem to find a quick and dirty solution is nice but if the problems comes back again and again afterwards, sometimes with increasing damage, it might not be the best idea to follow the Chinese way.

Since the creativity of one person is sometimes maybe a bit limited you might find out that if you call tech support or the janitor or anybody who is supposed to help you with technical issues they will not show up alone. They are mostly accompanied by other people who will all stand around, give (useless) advice to the one person who is working, and of course all of them want to get paid. After watching four masters of their business drilling a small hole in my wall or enjoying the view of three people changing a light bulb you might seriously get the impression that there are too many people here who have no idea what they are doing. Well, sometimes they know but they want to show off status – at some government organization I've met a higher manager who had an assistant who in turn had an assistant herself as well. Watching the show at breakfast was amazing: The assistant picks up the food and brings it to the manager, while the assistant of the assistant brings the food to the assistant.

Sometimes, you can see trucks driving around where they were too lazy or didn't have the right tools to make the transportation of goods safe – in the middle of the road there might be a truck where somebody is standing in the back and trying to make sure that the goods do not fall off by holding them with the bare hands.

Even at a middle-class restaurant you might be amazed how many service people there are when you are greeted by people behind the door who have exactly one task: Greeting new customers. Another waiter might bring you to your table and will wait patiently there until you finally chose your food, often supported by others since they think that they might understand what your needs are better this way.

What you should learn from this: For a specific problem there are always several solutions. With the right talent for improvisation, which you will surely get after a while, there will almost be no challenge anymore that you cannot surpass if you simply open your mind and start thinking simple and freely. And now at least you know that if you have no idea how to get something done it is totally acceptable to bring other people who are just as clueless as you are along with you.

25 Be Careful about Doing Business Here

In an economy growing like crazy it always seems like there are business opportunities everywhere. And yes, it might be even true. But you shouldn't take things too easy: Doing business here, especially if you are on your own, might involve much more risks than you could imagine at first.

It starts with the bureaucracy that might break your neck – and I am not only talking about getting the right chops from the right offices to get yourself started, e.g. getting the right visa. Never forget that as a foreigner you are much more high profile here than most Chinese people. Simply because they can get away with a lot of things they did wrong it does not necessarily mean you can, too. Even if you can for some time, the longer you do it the more probable it is that they will get you – punishments can be pretty harsh. Even if you fought yourself somehow through all the forms and stamps there might still be surprises waiting for you: Maybe some random office did not yet reach its quota of finding companies that did something wrong in order to collect fines, they might just show up at your company and tell you plainly that you have two choices. Either you will tell them something you did wrong yourself and they will fine you for it or they will tear your bookkeeping apart until they find something which will be much more trouble. These quotas can exist everywhere and you can simply be in a very unlucky position that they might hit you, e.g. if you are trying to change the location of your company. If you usually pay lots of taxes the local government office might not be too happy that you want to pay your taxes somewhere else from now on. You can be sure that they will find a way to postpone or even keep you from moving your office to another area. Another frequent example I've heard of several times is the "environmental license" that you need for a new plant and which is regularly postponing the opening.

Even if you somehow manage to survive all this bureaucracy did you ever wonder why all the companies have a security service here – even though the security guys do not really make anybody afraid anyway? They may be on site for 24 hours a day but probably sleeping all night so they do not really watch anything? What are they for if they don't do anything? Well, this might sound like a waste of money. But the consequence of not having security with low wages around might result in inconvenient visits of other people in your company trying to convince you that you really should hire their security guys – or something bad might happen afterwards.

Even if you don't do business on your own but you look for some Chinese people here helping you out: Finding high quality personnel is a hard task. Mostly they do not really fulfill the standards of what you have in mind and will need lots of training - and still they will find ways to do it wrong to make it easy for themselves. If business is running great anyway, that doesn't sound too bad. But always remember that as a general manager you are the legal representative of your company. And it could always happen that your employees do something not really great – and since you are the representative even if you did not do anything wrong in person you might end up in jail to prevent you from running away with little chances of leaving soon. And if this does not happen there are other issues at hand: Intellectual property rights, fluctuation of staff, not really streamlined processes, people not sharing their knowledge to make them more valuable, or people pretending to be really busy even though they rest their head on the table to sleep a bit if the boss accepts this or they sneak off to a room where they cannot be seen while sleeping if the boss doesn't agree with this habit.

AS you might have found out: I sneaked in a topic especially for foreigners since most Chinese will probably find a way how to handle these situations, they are used to it or they just do not care. But you as a Foreigner have a much higher profile and might run into problems much more quickly than locals. Just because you think this might be the new Wild West, where everybody is looking for Gold and might find it, does not mean there will be people left on the streets. Please do not be one of them.

Anyway, working in a company here is a small adventure on its own where you again will have a lot of interesting experiences – and lots of experiences where you just want to smash your head against the wall.

26 Lose All Interest in Politics

If you read the newspapers in your own country you will encounter a lot of negative aspects about China – especially the political system which does not include democracy and does not really take western values in consideration. While you are here you might get a completely different picture: People do not care.

And why should they? The communist party pulled out a whole country out of Stone Age and poverty within an extremely short period of time which might not have been possible this way if cared you too much about what the population thinks. With this party you have a very stable government which can work on its goals in a much longer term since nobody has to worry about getting elected again by the public. Of course they are internally also fighting for power while somebody putting somebody else in jail for corruption and other crimes, but mostly these battles happen behind closed doors. If you are not a party member there is probably no need for you to get involved in politics ever anyway – and probably if you are Chinese you already have lots of other issues to deal with, e.g. making your living (for the poorer ones) or getting even richer (for the not so poor ones).

And even I have to admit that the government is making lots of smart choices – by looking at other countries, checking what they did right and what they did wrong, imitating the right things and adjusting it in a way that it somehow almost always works. Until now the country still almost evaded every chance of a crash and I am very positive that they will do so in the future, too. With the censorship and other measures they make sure everybody stays in line on pushing the country forward which might not be so great for the people who want to think freely but which is great for the whole country itself. And sometimes people with higher ranks also gain profit from it, but still – this system works.

It is really amazing to see how the people are not interested in politics or at least can live with the consequences, even if it affects their personal life in a very direct way. Can you imagine that in your country everybody would simply accept that in a city of over 15 million people it would suddenly be forbidden for half the cars to drive – only to make sure the pollution goes down for some politicians from APEC or for the Olympic games so that these people can enjoy a blue sky? On a pretty short notice they put the system in place that on some days only cars with even numbers and on others only cars with odd numbers on their number plate can drive. Meanwhile, they also disallowed trucks from entering the city – a nightmare for the supply chain. But in other news they also sent government offices, schools, and government factories to a forced vacation with just a few weeks of short notice.

On other days they might send all foreign students on a mandatory school trip to make sure they are not in Beijing, if they think it is necessary for the harmony in the country. How do the people react? Well, it is a mix of enjoying the free time and taking it with dark humor. The blue sky of the APEC meeting was subtitled with "Air Pollution Eventually Controlled" and the good air of the Olympics got nicknamed "Olympic Blue". On the opposite there is a name for the cough you can get because of air pollution: "Beijing Cough".

There are some notable exceptions to the "Do not care"-Rule: As soon as you mention some sensitive topics your new friends might become a bit unhappy about. You should never criticize Mao Zedong who is still mostly highly appreciated. It might also be a bit strange to listen to taxi drivers, telling you some stories how great Adolf Hitler was since he was a strong leader. And you should also not comment on issues about Taiwan, Tibet, Hong Kong or other matters of domestic politics. And please also do not say anything about international diplomacy – even if nobody is really showing any interest in these topics in the beginning, this might suddenly change if you start mentioning your opinion.

If politics is not the profession you want to take in your future there is only one reason to join the communist party: It might help you a lot in your career since there are always good positions to be found in the companies that belong to the state where not only qualification is a criteria but also the connections you have in the party.

For everybody else: As long as the government still addresses and works on the issues that everybody meets in their daily life and finds some way to canalize the hidden frustration towards other countries there is absolutely no need to be ever interested in politics here. And you as a foreigner do not have any way of joining the communist party anyway.

27 Get Preferential Treatment

In a country with a population as big as this you might sometimes get the wish to put yourself ahead of the others. There are two ways to do this: Either by money or by a lot of influence. As much influence as a local government representative who was unsuccessful in negotiating for free alcohol in a KTV and therefore decided to switch off electricity for a whole district just to show the staff who was in charge. What you maybe could achieve as a foreigner working for a big company is VIP treatment for appointments at the local bank where you do not have to wait in line.

If you are not by chance the manager of some electricity grid or working for a big company you probably have to rely on your own money, and even there is much fun you can have: For many activities you can upgrade to a VIP or VVIP package. If you go to the barber, you can choose the skill of your haircutting guy from "student" to "technical director" with very different prices. In a restaurant you can take a private room. In theaters you can book better seats, which mostly do not bring a big advantage but cost much more. In the SPA of course there is a VIP treatment too. And even a visa application can be processed a lot quicker if you deliver enough money to the agent. And don't even get me started on students – Chinese universities often offer special dormitories for foreigners which are more expensive but have the following advantages: Single or Double room instead of living together with up to 7 other people in one room, private shower and bathroom, and being allowed to enter and leave the building 24/7. Of course this comes at a price. In some cases you may not have the right influence and cannot buy the preferential treatment directly, but you might know people who have influence and will help you out for a special courtesy: While paying money directly might be considered as consulting fee or illegal corruption you can also repay your favors by sending expensive gifts or making it possible for somebody to have a nice trip to another country for "training".

Even if you do not really know anyone you can still enjoy this treatment if you are happy enough to be invited as guest of a person with a lot of influence: As a guest of the local government and depending on your perceived importance as a guest you might enjoy a police or even military escort, or locked down locations for the public so that only you and your host can enjoy the place.

If you stay on the legal side all of these VIP treatments might sum up to a significant amount of money, and you can also invest in a customer card which is offered in many places: You buy a certain amount of credit, usually you get some kind of discount for it – and then you can use this prepaid credit to spend on services or goods. You can only as much as hope that the business you are investing in is still in business until you've spent the amount on your customer card.

And if you have no money and no influence and all other methods fail: Remember to be selfish and grab your preferential treatment. If you cannot find a parking spot for your car simply park in the middle of the road. When waiting in line is taking you too long cut it or make the process quicker by pushing yourself through. In a location with service shout at the poor people who are working there. Sometimes it works.

28 Re-Evaluate Risks and Stay in Your Comfort Zone

The world is a risky place, we all know that. What you probably did not see yet is where the real risks are.

Driving along a road on the countryside without light in the middle of the night is not risky, even if most of the trucks do not have lights either or if parts of the roads are broken down. Having sex without a condom is also not risky, neither because of illnesses nor because of getting pregnant. Kissing somebody else in front of the toilet while your boyfriend is waiting back at the table in the bar? Not risky.

No, the real risks lie in things like: Traveling alone somewhere, going out too long in the evening, participating in new activities that you've never heard of, learning to swim in a safe pool.

One of the reasons might be that thanks to the one-child-policy children are seen as an asset and are taken care of accordingly. Taken care of so much that they basically are allowed to do anything they want as long as the parent is there. Even here the locals did recognize this and found out that they are raising "little emperors". But thanks to all the taking-care-of children are basically not allowed to make their own decisions, their own mistakes, and their own experiences. And suddenly, after being the small emperor in a family for over 20 years they have to cope with life themselves. Imagine you have somebody at your side for your entire life, telling you what to do and what not to do, and then suddenly you find yourself on your own: How would that feel? While most of the foreigners you might meet here are pretty much used to leaving the comfort zone, e.g. living in a foreign country, being in situations that they did not know before and finding their own way through life including the evaluation of risks, people here do not really want to take a single step out of their comfort zone at all. Still, some of them are full of admiration for people who do but they would never try it themselves.

And if they somehow managed to get out of their comfort zone in one area they often get totally overconfident in there. As soon as the first weird feeling of driving a car is gone they like to speed up well above the level of their own control. This leads to the really weird situation that at least in my humble opinion there is a serious lack of risk calculation and balancing, and there is nothing like: "I have a bit of experience in this, I can do it maybe if I am careful". There is just an "I am the best in this" or an "I have never tried it and never want to". Sometimes accompanied by an "I would do it with parents" or another kind of expert.

Sometimes the same trust mechanisms work here that also work in other countries: If you want to make somebody believe that you are trustworthy pretend that you are a big fan of their hometown, that you know somebody living there or even better that you grew there up yourself. While the last one might be a bit hard to believe with your foreign face all of these methods might be used when Chinese bank employees sell investment products to lower the perceived level of risk of the customer. Either way, try to lower the perceived risk level by creating a personal bonding due to commonly shared experiences even if they are fake ones.

Some serious words of warning at the end: Do not trust people too easily here. Most people are really nice and treat you very well but if something seems too good to be true it most likely is, and also comes with a serious catch. The "tea scam" where beautiful girls talk to foreign guys to "exercise their English" is the start of an "invitation" to a tea house where you might end up with a bill of several thousand Renminbi and some strong guys enforcing you to pay the bill. Also, guys who might promise you a lady or a lady bar are not as trustworthy as you might think.

But hey, you could also be truly Chinese, completely forget about what risk is and follow them. I guess you will have an once-in-a-lifetime experience which at least I for my part do not want to have.

29 Be Traditional. Or Not.

Chinese people are proud of their long history and culture – and they are right, they really can be proud about it .Sadly there is a small problem with this: Their ancestors have this culture. And they themselves, well... let us just say that most people are a bit lost on the cultural highway and not really the most civilized ones. Still, traditions and old stories are highly valued, at least if it somehow fits to the personal preference. For Chinese New year tradition mandates that you should return to your family. On Moon festival you should eat moon cakes. On Valentine´s day you should buy flowers. On Halloween dress up and on Christmas.... Well, you will surely find an awful lot of decorations everywhere and find enough ways to spend money for this very new tradition.

If you ask me what a traditional Chinese girl is: No idea. If you ask a Chinese girl what type she is the answer will be very often: Traditional. And if you ask what "traditional" means in detail you will again find out that they basically do not have any idea either what that means. There are some ways of behavior which can show how traditional you are: Do not sleep around, best way would be to enter marriage as a virgin. And no worries if this hint comes too late for you, there are doctors here who have specialized in making you a virgin again with a small operation. Do not go home too late, do not smoke, do not drink, and do not go to bars.

As a truly traditional girl you should also make your husband work for you – while he earns the money you should take control of it and be the finance minister of your family. Before even getting married demand a house or an apartment as shelter even if you are not planning to live there at all.

One of the most interesting aspects of "traditional" girls is that they mostly are not as traditional as they try to show in public. As soon as nobody is around who knows them they sometimes change from shy girl to man-eating beast.

You will maybe recognize that in urban settings you are in a really modern world but the old beliefs are still strong here. When one of my classmates tried to take pictures inside the Ming Tombs our teacher was scared to death because she thought taking pictures in tombs might steal her soul and she begged us not to take a picture while she was around. When you meet new people, especially when you start dating, people will be awfully interested in your zodiac or in which year you were born, even the blood type sometimes seems to be an important factor to consider whether or not somebody is a potential soul mate. Some of the dating websites here also ask for your monthly income and other information that nobody would share in the western world to the public.

I guess being a traditional guy is a bit easier: Find somebody who will marry you if you bring enough money – but this is a topic for the next chapter. When you finally found a soulmate and somehow managed to get married to somebody you will have lots of traditional games to play at the wedding. And even before: Have some "traditional" wedding pictures taken. If you do not plan to get married here I still really recommend that you have a close look at the favorite locations of couples to take these kind of pictures. It is really amazing how people line up next to each other trying to pretend on the picture they are the only ones in that area and slag the other couples around off while waiting.

To show everybody that you are a civilized, traditional guy, you might also try to learn as many idioms as possible to sound wise.

30 Guys only: Give All the Money to the Girl

Yes, we talked about relationships already on the chapter about "being traditional". But this obviously is mostly only true for girls so here is the other side of the coin: Guys are cheaters. If you are not poor go visit one of the many prostitutes available in all the locations where the innocent foreigner would never expect them: Karaoke places where you can rent a beautiful girl to enjoy singing and more. Barber shops with not a single pair of scissors in there. On the street sometimes a girl will ask you about "massage". In the hotel, either by the lots of business cards somebody pushes through under the door or by the "you want a massage"-calls in the evening. Massage Salons with extras. Online. Wherever. If you are really rich, find a mistress and give her everything that she wants: House, car, expensive jewels. If you are even richer than really rich get yourself a second mistress - your bank account is the only limit. But wait a second – are the wives in this country really that stupid and they do not know that what you are doing?

Actually, they are not that stupid. Therefore Chinese culture invented something really great: Give all the money to the girl. When being married the woman has control over all finance issues – not because Chinese women are all financial geniuses but because a man is best controlled by limiting the money he can spend. And to make sure that you are actually broke before entering marriage: You cannot get married to a girl without owning an apartment or house. Girls will not accept this. Or their family will not accept it. That way it it's actually made sure that you spend all your precious cash that you might have on real estate, and you have to start over with her from a bank account balance of zero. But do not forget to have a secret income or savings for your affairs.

By the way: Apartment prices are ridiculously high here, especially in the first tier cities like Beijing or Shanghai: You think that in your hometown or in London you have to spend a lot of money to buy an apartment? If you compare the apartment prices here with the annual income you might be surprised how people manage to finance their own apartments over here. And I am not talking about exploding rents, I am also talking about the prices you have to pay for buying your own small or big home.

Even if you are lucky enough to find a girlfriend who does not expect you to buy a house for her you might find that feminism hasn't really reached the kingdom of the middle just yet: Being the guy you are responsible for paying all the bills that might arise during dating. Cinema, Restaurant, KTV – you name it. And do not forget the precious gifts that you should buy. It is not uncommon for not so rich students or the working population that the guys will spend a significant amount of their small income for dating. Sometimes the story doesn't end in happy marriage but in tragedy instead: There was a news story about a guy shopping at a mall with the girl for hours. After having a short argument with her, telling her he wants to go home now and her refusing since she wanted to continue to spend money, he obviously used the only way out that he could find: Jumping down from the seventh floor in the mall to his death.

I hope you find a better way to solve this problem.

31 Listen to Your Parents

Since social security is just slowly entering the Chinese system people have relied on their children in the past. The parents inspire you, decide for you, and they show you how to live your life. You should not argue with them, and what they say must surely be right.

Thus, if you think that you can choose your partner for yourself you are seriously mistaken. Also, do not think that you can follow your own timeline: Since you should focus on studying you should not date until university. And after university you should probably get married very soon. If a girl is around 26 years old the parents start to get worried in case she is still single. At around 30 she can expect that the mother will move in for a while to introduce her to some single guys around. If you are already 35 and not married yet you are obviously one of the left-over women and your parents gave up hope on you already.

If your parents also start to be Chinese they will do everything in order for you receive great education: Paying lots of money for an English training at kindergarten, giving you private teachers, and sending you to the best learning institutions they can afford and that you can get access too. They want to protect you and care about you even when you are already old enough to have children yourself. Why is that? Do they love you that much? Yes, that might be one reason. Or they just invest in their own future and try to make sure that somebody cares for them when they're old. And if you already have a child on your own it is pretty common for your parents to take care of it, giving you more than enough time and opportunity to earn enough money to finance their retirement. Since retirement age is early here (60 for men, 55 for women in the year 2014) they have a long way to go without a salary. That is why you exist – and thanks to the one-child-policy (which by the way has many exceptions) they have to rely only on you, if they did not make a fortune in another way.

Anyway, listening to your parents starts with a big first step: Do not move out of your parents' house. Stay there until you are married. And yes, of course staying out all night with your boyfriend or girlfriend – which is commonly seen as a first step to get married – will require lots of excuses and lies. If you somehow made the terrible mistake of moving out, for example for studying at university, and you have no other chance than to live at the local dormitory you still should go visit your parents regularly, especially every holiday. Call your parents regularly in the evening, tell them that everything is okay – and of course always answer their calls, which will sometimes come in the evening on an almost hourly basis.

Side note: If you want to be truly Chinese I guess your parents will need some training here. Just tell them that they should imagine you were still are a small kid, even if you already are in your thirties or older. Ask them to organize life for you.

While it is really comfortable to stay with your parents all day until you are finally married or able to move out you will have the next challenge in front of you. Since your parents always took care and solved all the big and small problems for you when you were young you will eventually face the one problem everyone faces at some point: You have to stand on your own feet and grow up. While in the western world this is often a process here it can suddenly hit you hard in the face.

32 Understand the Factors of Chinese Planning and Logic

As you might have figured while reading that topic, planning and logic do not really have anything in common with the western ways thereof. While many foreigners might misunderstand the local culture by saying there is no planning and logic at all – and yes, you will get that impression a lot – I do not agree with this. It is just very different here.

If you consider the first chapter then you will definitely find some connection: Planning and logic is mostly based on the "I come first"-worldview. And while people from other countries might plan a bit beforehand this will not always be the issue here. To make it really short: Forget about planning. Just look at what your needs are right now and try to fulfill them as quickly as possible or find somebody who can help you fulfill them. You've just left your hotel room, entered a travel bus and set off on a long journey? Demand that the driver stops right now because you have to go to the bathroom. Check-out-time in the hotel is 12:00 at noon, it is 11:50 and you recognize that you want to take a shower first because you forgot the time while watching TV? Tell the reception that you will stay in that hotel longer, free of charge of course. At work you get a task that doesn't bring you any pleasure? Try to push it off to somebody else even if that means that later on you'll have a very long chain of information from the first person who wants to have the task done towards the person who's actually doing it. Nobody would admit he delegated the task to someone else anyway. There might be some opportunity to shine with the great result in the end.

Since everybody here is used to new information and new requirements coming in all day, there is no need to really plan anything in advance. Plans change so quickly that you forget which plan was the current one anyway, so you have to be spontaneous to follow the flow that is happening around you. While in my old job in my home-country everything was planned through here it is impossible to even make plans for one day, since your colleagues, your boss or customers will pop into your office every few minutes and unload all the information and tasks that they have for you in mind. And they totally do not care about what you are doing right now or if it might be suitable for you or not. They might send you an e-mail and immediately pop in your office afterwards to ask if you are already working on it. Be prepared for the things that you cannot prepare. Forget planning. It is not worth it mostly.

If you are thinking about logic… what logic? I guess it might take you a while to understand the logic of the people here. Very often the so-called logic has to do with what other people do – if they do it, it must be right. And even if it is crystal clear to all Chinese, for a foreigner it might not be that logical after all. For instance, if you've ever considered buying an apartment or a house here you will have seen that the prices are way above of what you might have expected. One of the reasons will be that people buy real estate as an investment but do not live in there or rent it to others. Since property prices have been going up for years it is really convenient to just own one, even if it is not put to use. This lead to amazingly interesting cities like Ordos, which was designed for over a million people – but since all the apartments there are only for investment purposes merely 20.000 people are living there by 2014. And since especially the rich people mostly invest in real estate for most people there is no living space left that they can afford. But it is of course much more important for the rich to become richer with their empty apartments than giving poorer people a home. Illogical you say? From western point of logic, yes it is. Local Logic tells you otherwise.

In addition to the "I come first"-worldview the Chinese education system probably plays an important role as well – learning and studying is mostly based on memorizing. Logical thinking and/or considering causality is probably not the biggest strength in the local culture. If you memorize all the books and lectures character by character you might get great grades but it does not really help in being able to develop your own thoughts. Therefore, Chinese logic might by be logical in a very small frame and will fall apart as soon as you start to think "out of the box". But due to education this does not happen too often.

Since Chinese culture is really ancient and most inhabitants here are really proud of this there are some more factors which play a big role in plans, for example numbers. Considering that the number four sounds like "to die" it is not surprising that people do not want to have phone numbers with any fours in it? That nine sounds like "long" so that is why many people want to marry on the 9th of a month? And never forget the massively important May 20th, which remotely sounds like "I love you", so this must be a great day to celebrate with your boy- or girlfriend or send her gifts. The number eight reminds people about getting rich, leading to some hotels only providing rooms with numbers starting with an eight. And the number six means that everything will be smooth.

Next to the numbers you also might consider the Chinese calendar; this one also plays a big role in everyday life – which mostly consists of eating of course. During the moon-festival you should really eat moon-cakes, on some other days you should eat dumplings, and on your birthday really long noodles to represent your (hopefully) long life.

If you are just a tourist here I guess nobody will be angry with you if you do not know all this and do not consider these aspects in your otherwise non-existent planning. If you stay here longer and if you are not sure you really should get a Chinese consultant, especially if you want to do business. It would be a pity if your great business went down the drain simply because you should have planned beforehand JUST ONCE.

Again, as a rule of thumb I can give you the following advice to be Chinese: For beginners, if you want to be Chinese forget about logic and planning. Just follow your current needs and ideas without big planning.

For the advanced: Grab a good book about numbers, holidays, and Chinese culture in general and adopt it in your everyday life. But believe me you can get by very well without it.

33 Speed Up and Slow Down According to Your Needs

Take a look at the economic development of China in the last decades and you will see that the country is pushing forward. This is also reflected in every day's life: When I compare the speed of life in my own European home to China the pace is quite different here. Amazingly fast. Quick development can be seen in the economy but also in personal life in almost every aspect. People are rushing from one place to another supported by the environment: How many cities do you know where in a subway the average waiting time for the next train is just a few minutes? Where people are running around much like bees are flying around their hives?

Mostly, there is no need to make big plans in advance neither for private life nor for work since new developments might put a change to the plan even before it started developing.

No wonder that more and more local inhabitants feel big pressure and enjoy relaxing – either by staying at home and doing nothing but also on other occasions, like when taking a walk during lunch break. While sometimes people are running around like busy bees during lunch time they put on "slow mode" that even a snail might win against them in a race. This of course is just hypothetical – since probably mostly snails have something better to do and every animal should be a bit careful about showing up since there might be somebody around who wants to eat snails for dinner.

Also, for you this speed might be pretty influential for your life here. Things are changing all the time: While occasional visitors might see the change happening mostly in new construction sites being pulled up everywhere – and I certainly recommend having a look at the development of the Beijing Subway to get a good example – this lifestyle also influences daily life. Most people or companies are not really the most patient ones, meaning if they want to get something done they want to get it done immediately. Therefore, if you are working here do not wait too long with the tasks you got on your desk or otherwise you might lose a customer. Even if it is not your task to provide a service you should be sure that you make decisions quickly. If you want to rent an apartment or buy a ticket for a train you should buy it as quickly as possible since the apartment might either be gone or the train ticket might be sold out soon. Other people certainly do not wait for you until you've made your decision. And you should celebrate the times where you do not have any pressure – you will need this time to relax and calm down sometimes.

34 Don't Care About Animals –
but Love Pandas and Pets!

Open a bit your eyes and you will see a lot of poor animals in very poor living conditions: in the fish restaurant the crabs, fishes, turtles and other creatures are pushed into the aquarium, sharing it with dead specimen of their kind. On the streets you can sometimes buy a broad spectrum of animals put into a plastic bag or other container, sometimes even with colored water, where the poor creatures for sure will suffocate or at least die of hunger not too long time after. And there is still the occasional zoo where the poor animals are sitting with a blank stare because their cages are way too small. All of these are just a small part of the very obvious animal abusement happening on a daily basis. I guess you do not even want to know how the transports look like, in which the meat for your dinner is being transported – or the farms, where they sometimes grow up. If you still cannot imagine how animals are treated, you just can fire up a search on the internet and look for poor dogs which are pulled out of their fur while still being alive or cages thrown on the floor while the animals inside are weeping because of broken bones. Really cruel.

It is pretty obvious that people do not too much care about animals and their well-being, but there are two exceptions: Number one are the worldwide appreciated and not really common Pandas. Cuddly and cute they became a big international trademark for China – since there is basically no other place where you can see them. These small little bears get all what they need and do not need: Enough food, lots of space, lots and lots of toys which they totally do not need since they mostly sleep anyway – and even panda porn to support their breeding. Since these small cuties are that popular they have their own industry – providing panda hats, panda teddy bears, panda backpacks, panda whatever-you-can-think off. If you checked a bit the development during the last few years, there is another trend pretty obvious: More and more people get a pet, dogs being the most popular one. And this dog is treated like the own child – it mostly gets what it wants, people protect it and mostly do not really educate it very well. You cannot imagine how many misbehaving dogs I have seen here – and how often I listened to the complaints of the owners who have no idea how to educate their pet that the dogs basically bite everything into pieces.

35 Put Pictures on Social Media the Chinese way

If at some point you are that much integrated into the country that you have local friends – not only in reality, but also in social media – you will easily run into all of the pictures your Chinese friends are taking. It is always a pleasure to read the posts there. But even more pleasurable is it to check out the pictures you can find there. In general you can put them into five different categories: Food pictures, Selfies, I-am-so-great, I-am-so-poor and others.

I guess when you have a look at these categories, maybe you will not recognize that much difference from your own country – but the way of presentation might be a bit different.

As we already found out, Chinese people love food. So at least 30% of the pictures I can find in the postings of my friends in social media are about food. Local food, foreign food, fusion food, it does not really matter: But eating, as we already know, is important. And sharing what you are eating can also be considered importing, so start taking pictures of it.

Number two on the list are the so called Selfies, pictures you have taken about yourself. While this trend probably is on the rise in most countries, here it has some special points you have to take care of: Use some filter to make yourself look better. Much better. And if using a filter is not enough, use a software like Photoshop to increase your beauty. Since it is so popular, Photoshop even found its way into the slang with its abbreviation "PS" – this is especially worth mentioning since there are no equivalent syllables in Chinese. But before being able to use PS or a filter you first have to check the right motive – and since the background is sometimes pretty random you should probably focus more on your body language: Try to make your eyes as big as possible by all what your muscles and different camera angles can offer (yes, there sometimes are really creepy pictures of some girls who tried to do this). And if you are not trying to take a I-wanna-be-cute-picture you should at least show a cool pose, mostly including the popular "Victory"-sign that you can show with your hand. Number three are the "I am so great"-pictures that do not really look very different from other countries – maybe just a little bit on another scale. While in other places people maybe want to show that they got up the Mount Everest by climbing up in a record time, here people are a little bit more laid-back in the way they are showing off: Mostly it is about some kind of party (Social life!) or about some amazing achievement (which might be a little bit small on western scale sometimes).

A little bit more on the extreme are the "I am so poor"-pictures which are maybe a bit more extreme than you might be used to in the western world. Especially popular is the picture of the own arm while getting an infusion which represents some kind of serious sickness since all non-serious sicknesses can be cured by drinking hot water anyway. Well, this will only make an impression to you if you do not know that one of the standard procedures in the hospital seems to be an infusion – even when western doctors would probably just recommend some hours of rest in bed.

And finally there is the "Other" category with… well… everything else.

Since you now know how to make great pictures: Take some pictures showing the "Victory"-sign as a selfie while eating some strange food (Yes! You feel so good!) – and afterwards some pictures while getting an infusion in the next Chinese hospital to get some sympathy. Meanwhile you can also send some random pictures about some wanna-be-deep-topics like: the cold feelings of a refrigerator or the hard life of a rock. And still you will get lots of fans who will like these postings… As I said. Not so different from the western world.

Some Final Words

Congratulations! You've finally arrived at the end of this guide and are truly on your way to become a Chinese! Are your ready for the amazing journey to experience al of these aspects in person? And still I am sure that you will find lots and lots of aspects that might not have been covered in this book. But I am convinced I gave you a good foundation to just go out there and enjoy this country first hand!

At least for myself I have found my temporary home here, sometimes filled with joy and sometimes filled with anger about some of the local customs. But at least it is always a small adventure – and you never know how it will go on.

While writing this book I had lots and lots of ideas: And even after spending so much time on writing it, there are still many aspects missing. But putting such a diverse country in just a couple of pages to give you a crash-course is quite a challenge – so I sadly hat to stick to the most important points and leave out some personal notes, e.g. how much I enjoy the sometimes weird signs and translation problems (keep your eyes open while being in China!).

Anyway, since everything is changing here so fast – some of the information might be outdated already in a few years. But you should be prepared well enough now to adapt!

You cannot wait to put all your knowledge to the test? As final words, here are my two suggestions how to do this:

1. Do you still remember the first task? After arriving at this point, go back to the description about the "ordinary business trip" and keep it as a reminder about most of the points which are covered in here.

2. Book a flight, get a visa, come here and enjoy the madness!

Thanks!

My biggest thanks to Martin J. for helping me out on proof-reading this book and "harmonizing" the text – you cannot imagine how much I appreciate!

Of course thanks to my family for letting me grow up in a very non-Chinese way by allowing me to leave my comfort zone during my childhood a lot.

Matthias, who is always good for some short trips and beers in the evening to discuss private matters and business.

My Russian bears – What would I do without you?

My dear Pillow, who always supported and inspired me.

The organization that sent me here to learn more about the language and business culture, and especially great thanks to their local project manager who always supported me and was a great source of information.

My two professors, who supported the application to this program (otherwise I would probably still be stuck in Europe).

The old friends that I have left in my home-country but still did not forget me – and the new friends that I met here and taught me a lot about different cultures.

And of course especially thanks to you for buying this book. Keep up the good work – and there might be more to buy in the future.

www.ingramcontent.com/pod-product-compliance
Lightning Source LLC
Chambersburg PA
CBHW061654250726
48659CB00004B/1492